SOUTH DEVON COLLEGE LIBRARY

* 6 8 2 1 9 *

LITM DR MSN

Children First

A Study of Hospital Services

LONDON: HMSO

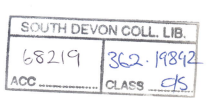

SOUTH DEVON COLL. LIB.
68219 | 362.19892
ACC | CLASS

© Crown copyright 1993

Applications for reproduction should be made to HMSO
Third impression 1995

Printed in the UK for the Audit Commission at Press on Printers
ISBN 011 886 096 8

London : HMSO

Audit Commission, National Health Service Report No.7

Preface

The Audit Commission is responsible for the audit of the National Health Service (NHS) in England and Wales. The Commission's auditors are required to review the financial accounts of all health service bodies and to examine the economy, efficiency and effectiveness with which they use resources. Each year a number of reports are published on health topics researched at national level. Local audits are then carried out on each topic.

The national reports are not intended to be comprehensive surveys because most of the detailed information will be collected in the audits that follow their publication. They are meant to highlight the national issues found in the study. When the audits are complete the Commission may publish a national summary of their findings.

The national studies are carried out by a team consisting of professionals relevant to the subject. They involve detailed examination of a number of study sites, the synthesis of published research and analysis of national data. The study team is supported by an advisory group consisting of individuals with a close interest in the subject.

The study of hospital services for sick children was lead by John Bailey and the study team included: Keith Dodd (Consultant Paediatrician), Jo Rodin (Action for Sick Children), Philip Blake, Penelope Eames and Ellen Ho. It was under the general direction of Ken Sneath. A full list of the Advisory Group and other contacts is given in appendix 1. The Audit Commission is very grateful for their help.

Table of Contents

Summary

Ten per cent of expenditure on hospital and community health services (about £1,400m) is on children. Although there are well-established principles for the care of children in hospital going back at least as far as the Platt Report of 1959, they are sometimes not implemented. Moreover, the effectiveness of treatments and the need for children to be in hospital are often not questioned.

This report does not seek to re-write the principles, but to investigate why they are not being met. Six main principles of caring for children in hospital are identified: child and family-centred care, specially skilled staff, separate facilities, effective treatments, appropriate hospitalisation and strategic commissioning. The report looks at each principle in turn, identifying the barriers in the way of achieving good practice and suggesting means of overcoming them. Examples are given where the need for change is clear and where immediate action can be taken.

Children have special health care needs because they are physically and emotionally different from adults and they need constant care and support from their parents. The root cause of hospitals failing to apply the principles is often a lack of attention of many clinicians, managers and other staff to these special needs and the needs of children's families. The solution is mainly to change attitudes and management practices. Some additional expenditure may be needed to take advantage of developments in methods of care, but it can often be found from abandoning inefficient and obsolete practices.

There should be a senior management focus for children's services in every hospital to ensure that the special needs of children and families are recognised in all aspects of care. Written policies that make standards clear to all concerned are needed, as are key indicators that are capable of being monitored.

Children should receive care from specially skilled staff and in facilities which are specifically designed to meet their needs. Experienced medical staff and Registered Sick Children's Nurses (RSCNs) are essential, but sometimes lacking. Improvements in staffing to meet these needs can often be made at little or no cost by reallocating or replacing existing staff. Also, separate facilities for children are often more cost effective because the range of tasks undertaken by staff is more concentrated and there is less duplication of equipment and materials. The problem in some areas is not the lack of separate facilities but insufficient use being made of facilities which already exist.

There is strong evidence in some areas of care (for example, cancer and intensive care of some newborn babies) that the special skills of staff at large tertiary or regional centres can achieve better outcomes at lower cost than at smaller general hospitals. There is evidence that mortality rates for very low birthweight babies receiving intensive care at large centres can be half those observed at local centres, and the average cost of providing that care can be as much as 30% less.

The outcomes of many treatments for which children are admitted to hospital are not routinely monitored. The report illustrates this using the management of glue ear (a condition which affects large numbers of children) and intensive care of newborn babies (a high cost service). Guidelines are recommended for monitoring outcomes for these services, which should be implemented in all hospitals.

Even though the amount of time most children spend in hospital has been falling over recent years there is still wide variation in admission rates and length of stay. The use of beds sometimes reflects their availability rather than a careful assessment of children's needs. There is a lack of clear guidance on when an admission is appropriate and a lack of consideration of the alternatives. For example, only 6% to 7% of newborn babies are admitted to special care baby units at some hospitals. If all hospitals reduced their admission rates to these levels, the total number of admissions to special care would fall nationally by about a third.

Children are sometimes kept in hospital unnecessarily because of administrative delays in arranging discharge, or a lack of services which can provide care at home. There is a potential for reducing bed numbers in children's wards and using the resources released to develop other services such as home care.

Health Authorities that commission health care have an important role to play. They set the broad strategy in which services should operate, providing a major catalyst for change. They should ensure that strategies are in place which address the key issues highlighted in this report.

Introduction

1. Health care services for children have developed rapidly over recent years as a result of:-

— **Changing health care needs**. Children who only a decade ago would have died are now surviving because of developments in medical and surgical techniques. Some require long-term support at home as well as repeated hospital care.

— **New approaches to the care of children in hospital**. The increasing emphasis on child and family-centred care and on involvement of parents in the care of their child has had a major impact on the quality of care offered to children and in particular on the role of children's nurses.

— **More care at home.** The need to keep children out of hospital because of the emotional stress it causes has been well recognised for the last thirty years. The provision of services to meet this need has only recently gained momentum with moves throughout the National Health Service (NHS) for more care at home.

2. In 1990/91, hospital and community health services (HCHS) for children accounted for £1,414m – about 10% of the total expenditure on HCHS for all ages (Exhibit 1, overleaf). Hospital services are estimated to comprise about half this expenditure; community services, ambulance services and administration make up the rest.

3. Child health services include the prevention of illness as well as its treatment and involve many different parts of the NHS. It is important that:

— the role of each part is clear to the children and parents using the services as well as to the staff involved;

— the services are provided in a co-ordinated and consistent way;

— wasteful duplication and inefficient use of resources is avoided.

This is what is meant by the concept of an 'integrated child health service' (appendix 2) which is widely accepted by the Department of Health, the Welsh Office and many of the professional bodies, as a guiding principle which should underlie all child health services. The Audit Commission endorses this view.

4. One of the key aims of the Audit Commission in looking at child health services is to examine the extent to which integration is working in practice. The Commission is undertaking two separate audits which cover a large part of the child health services. The first, which is the subject of this report, concentrates on the treatment of children in hospital. The second audit, which is due for completion in 1993/94, will focus on health promotion, disease prevention and child protection services and include the role of both health services and local authorities. The two studies overlap because health promotion, disease prevention and child protection services have an important role to play in reducing the need for health care, and the hospital services are (or should be) involved in these activities.

Exhibit 1

EXPENDITURE ON HOSPITAL AND COMMUNITY HEALTH SERVICES, ENGLAND 1990/91.

Children account for about 10% of HCHS expenditure.

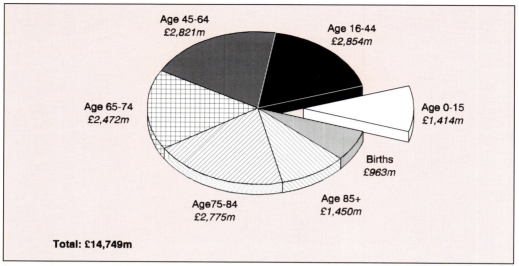

Age 45-64 £2,821m

Age 16-44 £2,854m

Age 65-74 £2,472m

Age 0-15 £1,414m

Births £963m

Age 75-84 £2,775m

Age 85+ £1,450m

Total: £14,749m

Source: Department of Health.

SCOPE OF THE STUDY

5. This study is concerned with the needs of all children from newborn babies to young adults. It includes anyone aged up to and including 18 years. Many health authorities and trusts set their upper age limit for children's services below this and run the risk of overlooking the special needs of adolescents.

6. Health care services for sick children may be described as a hierarchy consisting of 4 main levels of care (Exhibit 2). At the first level, most care of sick children is provided solely by parents. When further medical advice is needed, general practitioners (GPs) are usually the first contact (primary care). If a child who is ill cannot be treated by the primary care team they will be referred to a consultant. Secondary care in a general hospital follows referral from a GP, a hospital accident and emergency (A&E) department or maternity department. Tertiary care in a specialised centre takes referrals from general hospitals or direct from GPs. Examples include: cardiology services, cancer services, specialised paediatric surgery and intensive care. In addition to these four levels, there are the national centres such as those providing organ transplant services.

7. Although fewer children come into contact with secondary and tertiary care than with primary care, the average cost of treating them is much greater (Exhibit 2). This study concentrates on these two levels (excluding services for children who are mentally ill), but it also encompasses the links with primary care.

8. Most secondary and tertiary care takes place in hospital, but a growing proportion is now provided at home. Home care is especially preferable for children because it avoids the need for them to cope with the alien environment of a hospital as well as their medical condition. Home care is also often more cost effective (page 54).

4

Exhibit 2
LEVELS OF CARE.
Although far fewer children come into contact with secondary and tertiary care than with primary care, the average cost of treating them is much greater.

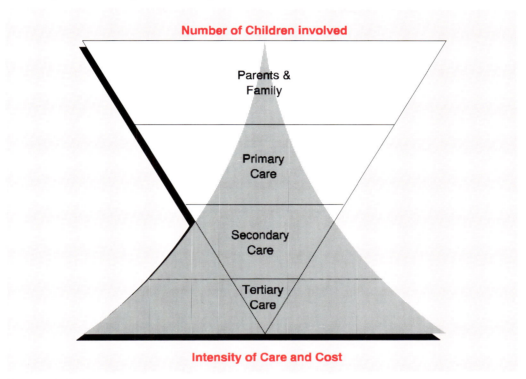

Number of Children involved

Parents & Family

Primary Care

Secondary Care

Tertiary Care

Intensity of Care and Cost

Source: Audit Commission.

TREATMENT OF CHILDREN IN HOSPITAL

9. There are about 14 million children and young people aged 18 and under in England and Wales – 28% of the population. In-patient admissions occur at the rate of about 1 per 11 children per year, amounting to about 16% of all in-patient admissions to hospital. Forty-two percent of them are under the care of paediatricians (Exhibit 3, overleaf); most of the remaining admissions (44%) are to eight surgical specialties. A large proportion of admissions to paediatrics – a medical specialty – are children aged under 1 year, whereas children admitted to surgical specialties are more evenly spread across the age groups, although there is a peak at 5 years due to ear, nose and throat (ENT) surgery. Almost all admissions in paediatrics are emergencies, compared to about two-thirds of children admitted for surgery. Most surgery on children is carried out by surgeons who also operate on adults. Only a small proportion is performed by paediatric surgeons who specialise in surgery for children, predominantly very young babies. The average length of stay of children in hospital is currently about 4 days (page 43).

10. Children also attend hospital as day cases, out-patients or 'ward attenders' (effectively out-patients who attend at short notice) – all categories of care which do not involve an overnight stay. But for many children, their first contact with the hospital is an A&E department. About 1 child in 4 in the population attends A&E in any one year (Ref. 1).

Exhibit 3
CHILD IN-PATIENTS AGED 0-18, BY SPECIALITY, ENGLAND AND WALES 1990/91.

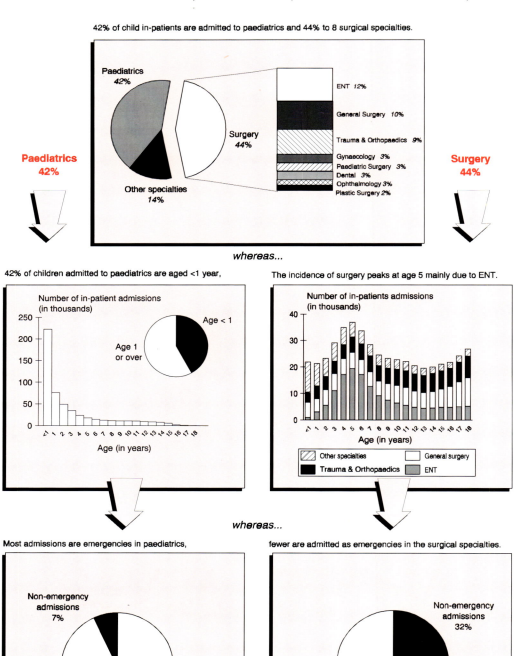

42% of child in-patients are admitted to paediatrics and 44% to 8 surgical specialties.

Paediatrics
42%

Surgery
44%

Other specialties
14%

ENT 12%

General Surgery 10%

Trauma & Orthopaedics 9%

Gynaecology 3%
Paediatric Surgery 3%
Dental 3%
Ophthalmology 3%
Plastic Surgery 2%

Paediatrics 42%

Surgery 44%

whereas...

42% of children admitted to paediatrics are aged <1 year,

Number of in-patient admissions (in thousands)

Age < 1

Age 1 or over

Age (in years)

The incidence of surgery peaks at age 5 mainly due to ENT.

Number of in-patients admissions (in thousands)

Age (in years)

Other specialties   General surgery
Trauma & Orthopaedics   ENT

whereas...

Most admissions are emergencies in paediatrics,

Non-emergency admissions
7%

Emergency admissions
93%

fewer are admitted as emergencies in the surgical specialties.

Non-emergency admissions
32%

Emergency admissions
68%

Note: (i)   Excludes normal healthy babies born in hospital.
*   (ii)   The term 'paediatrics' in this report refers to the medical specialty.*
Source: Audit Commission analysis of national data.

6

FOCUS OF THE REPORT

11. The Audit Commission has identified six principles which should underlie the care of sick children in hospital (Exhibit 4). These principles have evolved over the last 30 years or so, as a result of research and recommendations from various bodies. For example, the Platt Report on the care of children in hospital (Ref. 2) published in 1959, recommended principles of care for children in hospital, and in particular that children should only be treated in hospital if the treatment was not feasible elsewhere. The National Association for the Welfare of Children in Hospital (NAWCH, now called Action for Sick Children) was launched soon after the Platt Report to campaign for improved services. A major study of child health services as a whole was carried out in the early 1970s under the chairmanship of Professor Donald Court. The Court Report (Ref. 3) recommended in 1976 that community services for all children should be expanded and emphasised the need for much better co-ordination between existing services. The Department of Health published a new guide on the 'Welfare of Children and Young People in Hospital' in 1991 (Ref. 4). It was issued by the NHS Management Executive with the recommendation that it should form the basis of health service contracts for the provision of children's services.

Exhibit 4
THE PRINCIPLES WHICH SHOULD UNDERLIE SERVICES FOR SICK CHILDREN.
These six principles form the structure of the report.

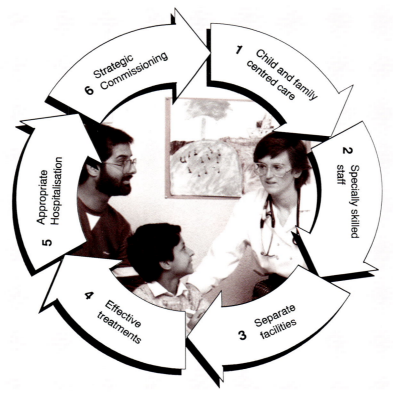

Source: Audit Commission.

12. Although the principles which should underlie health care for children are agreed by national bodies, there is a lack of awareness of them and of their importance at local level, resulting in poor implementation in some hospitals. This report does not seek to re-write the principles, but to investigate the extent to which they are not being met and to recommend ways of implementing them. The Department of Health's guidelines (Ref. 4), should act as a companion volume to this report. The chapters which follow look at each of the principles (Exhibit 4) in turn, summarising what is involved, identifying the barriers in the way of achieving good practice and suggesting means of overcoming these barriers. Examples are given where the need for change is clear and where immediate action can be taken. A glossary of terms is included.

13. In some hospitals, children's services are characterised by a pioneering and innovative approach which is driven by the needs of the children and which stands out from the rest of the NHS. Several examples of good practices were found at the study sites and these are cited, together with examples from other countries. But this approach is by no means common in every hospital. The aim of this report is to bring the performance of all hospitals up to the levels of the best.

1. Child and Family-centred Care

THE PRINCIPLES

14. The health care needs of children are different from those of adults:

— **childhood is a period of rapid growth and development.** Children of different ages have very different medical and surgical needs. They require an approach in day-to-day care which takes account of differences in their physical and emotional maturity;

— **children are part of a family and are dependent on their parents for physical and emotional care and support.** Caring for a child means involving parents and siblings.

Attention should be given to the needs of children for care and support, as much as to their medical or surgical needs. Children are less understanding than adults of the tendency of many hospital staff to focus on the condition rather the person. A more holistic approach to hospital care would benefit many patients, but for children its absence can result in bad experiences which may slow recovery, affect their emotional and social development and even have long term effects into adulthood.

15. Robertson (Ref. 5) showed that children in hospital who are separated from their mothers are likely to suffer more psychological stress and recover more slowly, than children whose mothers stay with them. This has gained considerable support from subsequent research. The stress is greater:

— if the child is aged under 5 years;

— the longer they stay in hospital;

— the more frequently they are admitted.

Close and continuous involvement of a child's family is now a key principle of child and family-centred care.

16. Many young children perceive the pain of hospital treatment and separation from their familiar environment as a punishment. Explaining what will happen using play can help young children prepare for hospital care by giving them greater confidence in the staff and understanding of the treatment. Play can also help staff understand the child.

17. For older children and young adults a different approach is required, recognising their needs for counselling, emotional support, peer group contact and a greater degree of involvement in decisions about all aspects of their care. A child's right to be involved in these decisions is a major principle of the Children Act 1989. Adolescents who are chronically ill will need to transfer to the care of adult specialists in their late teens. This can be a particularly difficult transition for them and needs to be handled sensitively by, for example, consultants in the specialities concerned holding joint out-patient clinics over a transitional period.

9

18. There are special cases where a more specific approach to care is necessary. For example: a child in need of protection, a child and family from an ethnic, religious or cultural minority group and in the event of the sudden death of a child, when care will need to focus on parents and siblings.

THE PROBLEMS

19. The root problem identified in the Audit Commission study is that **clinicians, managers and other staff do not give sufficient attention to the needs of children and their families.** It is manifest in a lack of written policies, management focus and poor communication between staff and parents.

LACK OF WRITTEN POLICIES AND MANAGEMENT FOCUS

20. Written policies are essential to ensure that requirements for child and family-centred care are understood by all those involved and applied consistently throughout the hospital. Often such policies do not exist. Where they do exist, they seldom state clearly the standards to be adopted in the hospital or who should be responsible for co-ordinating them and carrying them out. This is because the practices have been developed in an ad hoc way by enthusiastic staff, primarily paediatricians and nurses, with little or no input from senior management. Although the quality of care achieved by these staff may be high, there is no consistency in this from one ward or department in the hospital to another. For example, parents may be actively encouraged to participate in care in one children's ward, but left as bystanders in another ward in the same hospital. Again, some ward staff may encourage play, but the need may be ignored in the A&E department or the orthoptic out-patient clinic. Parents and children find these differences confusing and unjustifiable. The problem is not confined to general hospitals, where most children are treated, but also occurs in some children's hospitals.

POOR COMMUNICATION BETWEEN STAFF AND FAMILIES

21. Although the staff on wards which admit children often say, when asked, that they encourage parents to stay, this is not always made clear in the information leaflets and it is even rarer to find clear notices in the wards reinforcing the point. In a survey of 48 families of children with asthma, diabetes or cystic fibrosis, many parents often felt their role on the ward was unclear and that their experience in caring for their child was sometimes ignored (Box A). Both parents and children felt that they had little role in decisions about their care.

22. The Patient's Charter (Ref. 6) states that every patient should have a named qualified nurse to look after them and provide continuity of care. In a sample of 47 wards which admit children – including child and adult wards, none had a policy of allocating a named nurse for the duration of stay of all children (primary nursing). Staff on 41 (87%) of the wards said they had a policy of allocating a named nurse to a child for the duration of a shift, but even this limited attempt to implement the policy did not appear to be working in some cases. Tangible evidence of the implementation of this policy, such as a notice prominently displaying the name of the nurse for a child or parent to see, was found in only about half of the wards.

INVOLVEMENT OF PARENTS AND CHILDREN IN THEIR CARE.

A personal interview survey of 48 families of children with asthma, diabetes or cystic fibrosis was carried out as part of the Audit Commission study to investigate their needs and perceptions of services. The families were selected from the membership of voluntary groups concerned with each disease and represented a wide cross section of social groups and backgrounds.

Over half of the families reported that their involvement in care on the ward had been on the basis of a tacit understanding rather than explicit decisions. Some parents resented that their knowledge and experience in relation to their child was sometimes not recognised. The families had an average of 6.5 years experience of living with the disease.

'*I feel annoyed if expected to do less, because of continuity of the relationship (with the child). But I am not sure of their (the staff) attitude. …they let me do it so that they don't have to do it. I would rather see positive encouragement.*' (parent)

'*We took in all her medication. They took it from us and put it into a medical chest and we couldn't have a key. I had been taught to keep it in the fridge, but they said it wasn't possible. I was not happy with the situation*' (parent).

When asked why they felt they were included in the care of their child, 68% of parents in the sample gave reasons which can be grouped under the heading of 'providing support and reassurance to the child or continuity of care in a frightening situation', but 32% said their role was to substitute for a 'lack of staff'. This may mean that there are indeed shortages of staff, but it could also be indicative of a lack of clear policies or a failure on the part of the staff to communicate their policies to the parents.

Source: Audit Commission.

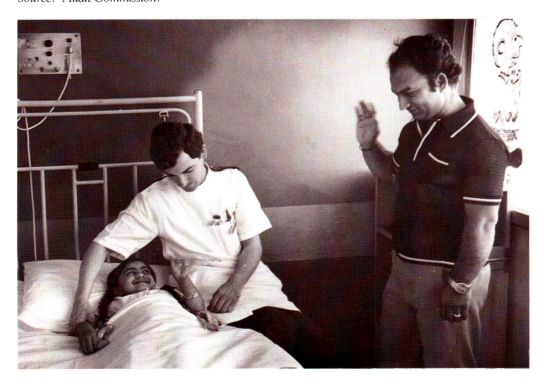

OVERCOMING THE PROBLEMS

23. Implementation of effective policies of child and family-centred care requires a major change in attitudes on the part of managers, doctors, nurses and other staff involved in running the service. This can be achieved in many hospitals at little or no additional cost. Even where additional training or staff time is needed to bring about change, this will in most cases be a transitory expense and in the long term the efficiency of services should improve. But changing attitudes is not something which can be done overnight. A much clearer management focus, a higher priority for children's services and written policies are needed to begin this process.

PROVIDING A MANAGEMENT FOCUS AND MAKING BETTER USE OF WRITTEN POLICIES

24. A specific management focus is needed for children's services in every hospital. As a minimum the management team should include:

— a consultant with overall responsibility for policies for all children's services;

— a senior children's nurse above ward sister level, to provide the focus for implementing consistent policies for the care of children in all parts of the hospital;

— appropriate managerial and financial support.

25. Senior managers should delegate authority to this management team to draw up a philosophy and an operational policy for implementing child and family-centred care. This involves (Ref. 7):

— defining and describing the key elements of the service;

— translating these into measurable criteria;

— setting target standards based on good practice, for example, those set out in appendix 3 and in other published documents (Refs. 4 and 9);

— identifying the individuals to be responsible for achievement of the standards;

— stating how progress will be monitored;

— measuring local performance against the standards.

26. The management team must have sufficient authority to implement its policies. One way of achieving this is to channel the budget for children's wards through it. This could also be extended to other areas of expenditure along the lines of a 'clinical directorate' for children's services. In many hospitals medical and nursing staff are already involved in management as part of a clinical directorate (Ref. 8). Establishing a management focus for children's services in these hospitals would involve a reorganisation of roles, rather than additional managerial responsibilities. However, it is important that clinicians are given adequate time to carry out their managerial duties and receive training in management methods.

27. Action for Sick Children has played a major role in developing standards for the quality of care of children in hospital (Ref. 10) and methods of monitoring these standards (Ref. 9). The Audit Commission has taken the principles of the Quality Review and developed them into a quality assessment tool which can be used by its auditors, and subsequently by the hospitals themselves. The development work has focussed on defining a relatively small number of indicators which can be measured from a range of different perspectives and applied consistently. Details are in appendix 3.

28. It is important that the assessments are independent. They should be carried out by staff who have the necessary knowledge and experience, but are not directly involved in providing the service. At the Portland Hospital, a private hospital for women and children in London, an annual assessment of the quality of care is carried out by independent consultants.

IMPROVING COMMUNICATION BETWEEN STAFF AND FAMILIES

29. A clearer management focus with written policies for child and family-centred care would be an important catalyst for improvements in day-to-day care. But improvements also depend on the firm foundations of good communications between the staff involved on the one hand, and between staff and families on the other. This includes staff at all levels: clinicians, nurses, managers and support staff. The role of nurses is particularly important because they have more contact with children and families than most other staff. There are three key areas in which change is needed:-

(i) Involvement of parents.

(ii) Named nurses.

(iii) Written information.

(i) Involvement of parents

30. Involvement of a child's family is a crucial part of their care. Staff need to recognise the importance of the parental role in hospital care and to encourage parents to be with their children at all times. This should include the A&E department, out-patient department, wards, anaesthetic rooms, X-ray facilities, and recovery rooms. Parents (and siblings) should also be encouraged to continue providing care and support for their child as they would at home, and to gain the knowledge and confidence to do more themselves. The knowledge and skills of parents of children with chronic illness should be recognised when they come into hospital. Many of these families will also need support to help them cope with the long term consequences of the illness both in hospital and at home (page 53) and advice from staff who are specially skilled to deal with their particular condition.

31. Involving parents in care requires commitment and time from specially skilled and experienced staff. But gaining the confidence of children and their parents, and teaching and supporting them to provide care themselves, may shorten hospital stays and prevent future admissions as well as improve the quality of care.

32. Involvement of families also depends on an appreciation of their specific needs. These needs differ according to the social, educational, ethnic, cultural and religious backgrounds of the families. Where necessary, interpreters should be available in the hospital to assist parents and their children. The Juliana Children's Hospital in The Hague, Netherlands, had access to a telephone interpreter service rather than employing interpreters directly.

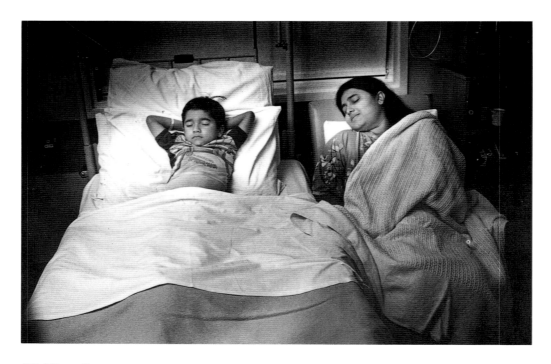

(ii) 'Named' nurses

33. Nurses play a major role in communicating with both parents and children. All hospitals should adopt a policy of allocating a named nurse to be responsible for the care of each child *throughout* their stay, and to provide a link with staff involved in post discharge care. This is a standard in the Patient's Charter (ref 6) which all hospitals should strive to achieve. The named nurse will not be able to provide all the care for an individual child, but should be responsible for planning and co-ordinating care provided by other nurses and support staff. The named nurse should also ensure that children and parents receive all the information they need. There is evidence from a previous Audit Commission study (ref 11) that wards with a policy of primary nursing do not generally have higher nursing establishments than other wards.

34. The same principle can be extended to A&E departments by having a 'named nurse' for each family for the duration of a shift. Similarly in out-patients departments, an effort should be made to allocate staff to regular clinics so that, as far as possible, they see the same families each time. Some hospitals are using nurses who also work on the ward (or day surgery unit) to cover out-patient appointments prior to a child being admitted for surgery. This means children can meet the ward staff in a less stressful environment than the ward, and there is continuity of care when they come for the operation.

(iii) Written information

35. Good personal communication and written information are equally important. Families need constant reassurance, time to take-in information and review what they have been told, and an opportunity to ask questions. Better information is required as parents become more involved in the care of their child. The main elements of the policy of child and family-centred care should be set out in information leaflets which are given to parents when they come to the hospital. All hospital departments dealing with children should, in addition, have a range of leaflets covering:

— policies specific to individual departments;

— the facilities and services offered in the hospital;

— details about the management of individual conditions and procedures;

— contact points for more information.

All staff involved in providing care should be involved in the preparation of this information. It is also important that appropriate information is given to families at different times: prior to admission, during their stay and at discharge, and that experienced staff are available to answer questions. This is particularly important for children diagnosed as having a life threatening or lifelong illness.

36. In the USA and Canada good quality information is a central part of management responsibility. As a result:

— production of information is co-ordinated;

— the quality of presentation is high;

— it is possible to find the information quickly and easily through the central information and retrieval system.

At the Washington Children's Medical Centre, all information produced has to be approved by a central multi-disciplinary committee, chaired by the Chief Executive. After approval by this committee, an inventory number is given and a timetable for review is agreed. The inventory contains an example of every piece of information approved, the names of the authors, the date of review and where it is stored.

37. The Hospital for Sick Children in Toronto has a Family Information Service open most of the day for children and their parents to drop in. It contains comprehensive information about the hospital, its services, specific illness, surgical procedures and other related topics. It also has information on health promotion and accident prevention for children which should be available in all hospitals. The centre has made arrangements for parents to have access to the medical library if they require more details.

38. It is wasteful of resources if every hospital is producing information from scratch. Certain commercial, professional and charitable organisations, produce information booklets which can be given to families by hospital staff, but they cannot deal with local issues. It would be useful if these organisations could produce information which can be easily adapted and extended to meet local needs by, for example, supplying it on computer discs or in loose-leaf formats. All hospitals should have part of their budgets set aside for producing information. It is often possible to obtain sponsorship from local businesses to provide high quality information leaflets in return for mentioning them in the leaflet.

2. Specially Skilled Staff

THE PRINCIPLES

39. The special needs of children and their families cannot be met without staff who have the right skills to:

— provide care and support for the whole family;

— deal with the highly specific problems of childhood illness.

THE PROBLEMS

40. The Audit Commission has identified two main problems in this area:

— some staff who care for children lack these special skills;

— children are not always referred for care at a tertiary centre when they need it.

LACK OF SPECIALLY SKILLED STAFF

41. Many staff are involved in the provision of health care for children: paediatricians, surgeons, nurses, play specialists, physiotherapists, dietitians, orthoptists, audiologists, health visitors, social workers, radiographers, phlebotomists and ancillary staff such as porters, cleaners and ward clerks. Some of these staff also provide health care for adults. All of them should be aware of the special needs of children and their families. This report focuses on paediatricians, surgeons and anaesthetists, nurses, and play specialists, because they see most children who come to hospital.

(i) Paediatricians

42. Over ninety per cent of children admitted to paediatric departments are emergency admissions. It is important that the medical staff who see these children are sufficiently skilled to offer effective help. First-line cover to wards is provided by senior house officers (SHOs) who are usually inexperienced in paediatrics. They should be supported at all times by more experienced junior doctors who provide 'safety net' cover and are resident on site. During normal working hours junior doctors can call on a consultant for assistance, but at night consultants are not resident on site. It is therefore important that the staff who provide resident cover at the hospital are sufficiently experienced to cope with emergencies. The British Paediatric Association (BPA) and the Royal College of Physicians recommend that junior doctors providing 'safety net' cover should have at least 12 months experience of working in paediatrics. According to data collected by the BPA in 1990, 16% of districts have no experienced junior staff and a further 8% are without these staff 'most of the time'.

43. Paediatricians provide the medical services not only to the children's wards, but to the A&E department, special care baby units and post-natal wards as well, and assist with the medical care of child surgical patients when necessary. The problems of providing sufficient cover are exacerbated when these departments are on separate sites.

44. The issue of medical staffing in general, including the needs for other grades of staff, is to be taken up by the Audit Commission in a forthcoming study.

(ii) Surgeons and anaesthetists

45. Children make up a relatively small proportion of the workload in acute surgical specialties other than ENT (Exhibit 5). If the work of an individual specialty is spread amongst several surgeons and anaesthetists, some of them may not deal with sufficient numbers of children to maintain the special skills, both in a professional sense and in communicating with children and their parents.

Exhibit 5
THE SHARE OF CHILDREN IN THE WORKLOAD OF 4 SURGICAL SPECIALTIES. IN-PATIENTS, AGED 0-18, ENGLAND AND WALES 1990/91.
Children make up a relatively small proportion of the workload in most surgical specialties, the main exception being ENT.

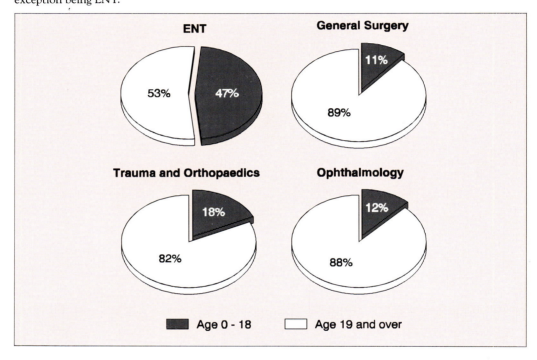

Source: Audit Commission analysis of national data.

46. The National Confidential Enquiry into Peri-Operative Deaths (NCEPOD–Ref. 12) carried out in 1989, included a sample of over 1000 surgeons and 2000 anaesthetists from England, Wales and Northern Ireland. Eighty seven percent of the surgeons said they operated on children. But 24% of those operating on children aged 3 – 10 years did fewer than 20 such operations per year and as many as 83% did fewer than 20 operations on children aged less than 6 months (Exhibit 6). Similarly in the case of anaesthetists (where almost all of them anaesthetised children), 15% said they anaesthetised fewer than 20 children per year aged 3 – 10 years and as many as 76% anaesthetised fewer than 20 children aged under 6 months. The conclusion of the enquiry was that:

'...*surgeons and anaesthetists should not undertake occasional paediatric practice. The outcome of surgery is related to the experience of the clinicians involved*'. *(Ref. 12)*.

Exhibit 6
THE INCIDENCE OF OCCASIONAL PRACTICE WITH CHILDREN AMONGST SURGEONS AND ANAESTHETISTS.
Many surgeons and anaesthetists deal with only a small number of children each year.

(a)   Surgeons

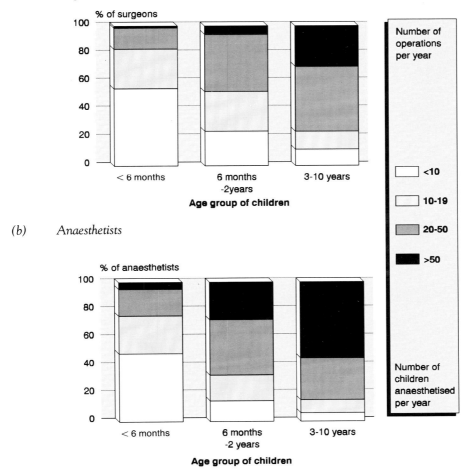

(b)   Anaesthetists

Source: Ref. 12.

(iii) Nurses

    47. Nursing children differs from nursing adults in two important respects:

— the skills required to nurse the child, such as in observation techniques and psychological support, are different;

— involving parents in care requires special skills in teaching and support.

In some areas of care, e.g. for children having haemo-dialysis, specialised surgery or intensive care, more specific nursing skills are required. A major study of nurses working in neonatal units is due to report in the next few months [1]. The basic qualification for nursing children is a Registered

---

1   *The Neonatal Unit as a Working Environment: A Study of Neonatal Nursing. Institute of Child Health, University of Bristol. Funded by the Department of Health.*

Sick Children's Nurse (RSCN). The Department of Health (DoH) has set a target standard which is that there should be:

"...at least 2 Registered Sick Children's Nurses - or nurses who have completed the child branch of Project 2000 – on duty 24 hours a day in all hospital children's departments and wards...and a RSCN on duty 24 hours a day to advise on the nursing of children in other departments...(Ref. 4).

48. Despite having RSCNs on their establishment, most wards are at times during the day staffed with only one RSCN, or occasionally none at all (Exhibit 7). The situation at night is even worse, with almost 50% of wards failing to meet the DoH standard on any shift (Exhibit 7).

Exhibit 7
USE OF CHILDREN'S NURSES IN A SAMPLE OF WARDS.
(Percent of shifts on each ward with 0, 1 and 2 or more RSCNs on duty).
(a)   Day shifts
         Most wards are at times during the day staffed with only one RSCN, or occasionally none at all.

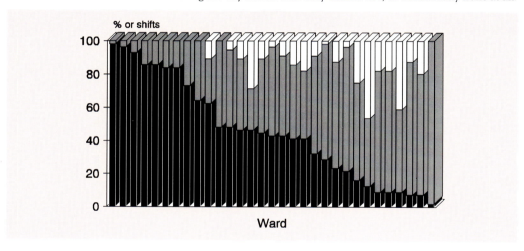

(b)   Night shifts
         Almost 50% of wards fail to meet the DoH standard on any shift at night.

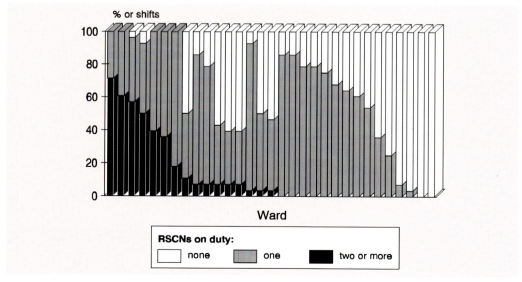

Source: Audit Commission survey of 31 wards in 7 hospitals.

20

These conclusions are based on sites selected partly because they were thought to be centres of good practice, so the national picture may be even worse. Some wards did not even consider the standard as an issue in rostering.

49. A major national study of career prospects for RSCNs, (Ref. 13) identified two main reasons for their scarcity:

— managers (both general and nurse managers) frequently do not perceive a need for RSCNs;

— the lack of prospects for career development in sick children's nursing and the low status of the work as perceived by nurses in general.

(iv) Play specialists

50. All staff should be aware of the purpose and need for play, but the major responsibility for organising play and overseeing its role ought to lie with play specialists. Thirty per cent of 34 wards surveyed at the study sites had less than 0.5 whole time equivalent trained play staff.

51. The definition of 'trained play staff' is not always clear. Some hospitals count nursery nurses and even volunteers as play staff. But they often have other duties as well as play. The Play in Hospital Liaison Committee define a play specialist as 'someone who has completed a course recognised by the Hospital Play Staff Examination Board' (Ref. 14).

POOR ACCESS TO TERTIARY SERVICES

52. Some childhood illness is very rare. The special skills necessary to treat it may only be available at tertiary centres where sufficient numbers of children can be seen for staff to develop these skills. There is well established evidence for the treatment of some cancers and for intensive care of very low birthweight babies (less than 1500 grams), that mortality is lower for children treated at tertiary centres rather than general hospitals.

Cancer

53. Survival rates are significantly higher with most forms of childhood cancer if they are treated at paediatric oncology centres (Ref. 15). In a sample of 3,000 children diagnosed as having cancer between 1981 and 1984, 25% were not treated at paediatric oncology centres. The rates of survival are significantly higher for the paediatric oncology centres (TABLE 1). Moreover these centres experienced a more rapid improvement in survival rates of children diagnosed over the period 1977 to 1984 than the secondary centres, further accentuating the gap between them. The benefits in terms of quality adjusted life-years (QALYs) gained from successful treatment of cancer in children are very large.

Table 1
PERCENTAGES OF CHILDREN WITH DIFFERENT DIAGNOSES WHO ARE ALIVE AFTER 3 YEARS ACCORDING TO WHERE THEY ARE TREATED. ORIGINAL DIAGNOSIS IN 1981 – 84.
Survival rates are significantly better at paediatric oncology centres.

	Treatment centre	
	Paediatric oncology centre	Other non-teaching centre*
Acute non-lymphoblastic leukaemia	32	6
Non-Hodgkin's lymphoma	70	58
Ewing's tumor	50	45

* All differences are significant at the 5% level.
Source: (Ref. 15).

Intensive care of very low-birthweight babies

54. Survival of babies born before 28 weeks gestation is better in large tertiary level neonatal units than in smaller units at general hospitals, even though the tertiary units are dealing with sicker babies (Ref. 16). In a sample of 102 babies, 64% received care at large tertiary units, the remaining 36% at smaller secondary level units. Fifty-two per cent of those at the large tertiary centres survived, compared to only 22% at the secondary units. This is supported by evidence from other countries (Refs. 17 and 18).

55. Most if not all babies of less than 28 weeks gestation or less than 1500g at birth will require a period of intensive care. For the purposes of this study intensive care is defined as: '*care given in an intensive care nursery which provides continuous skilled supervision by qualified and specially trained nursing and medical staff...*' (Ref. 19) and involving assisted ventilation. A recent study estimated the cost of providing intensive care per baby per day as £640 in units providing 1000 occupied cot days at all levels of care (adjusted to 1991 prices), but as only £450 per day at units providing 5000 days per year, a difference of 20% (Ref. 20)[1]. These costs include most of the costs of transporting the babies to tertiary units because staff from these units often collect babies.

---

1   *A more detailed national study to include 60 hospitals is being co-ordinated by Dr W Tarnow-Mordi of the Department of Child Health at the University of Dundee. The project is supported by the Medical Research Council.*

56. Whilst it is true that the majority of babies in need of intensive care receive it at tertiary centres there is evidence of an increasing tendency to decentralise services (appendix 4). It is driven mainly by arguments that costs are lower and the quality of care is just as good. This goes against the available evidence.

Other tertiary services

57. There are parallels with these arguments for other services, such as paediatric intensive care. Children aged over 4 weeks requiring intensive care may be admitted either to specialised paediatric intensive care units, or to intensive care units at general hospitals, which also care for adults. Although there have not been any detailed studies of differences in outcomes between these types of units in the UK, there is evidence from the USA that survival rates can be as much as 4 times higher at tertiary units (Ref. 21).

58. For some children requiring emergency surgery, the dangers of '...*occasional paediatric practice*' cited in the NCEPOD report (Ref. 12) imply that the necessary skills may only be available at tertiary centres. The differences in the likelihood of complications at tertiary and secondary centres following surgery are cited in a recent paper (Ref. 22), but there is an urgent need for more detailed studies comparing outcomes and costs.

OVERCOMING THE PROBLEMS
PROVIDING MORE SPECIALLY SKILLED STAFF

59. Specific problems were identified with four main categories of staff: paediatricians, surgeons and anaesthetists, nurses and play specialists.

(i) Paediatricians

60. There is a need to provide paediatric medical staff with sufficient experience for emergency cover where this cover is currently inadequate. GPs are taking over much of the work of Clinical Medical Officers (CMOs - doctors who work mainly in the community) in the areas of primary care pre-school child health surveillance, disease prevention and health promotion. CMOs are increasingly working in hospital as well as in the community, sometimes providing secondary care as part of a 'combined child health service' which spans both hospital and community health services (Ref. 23 and appendix 2). Most junior doctors working in paediatrics in a training grade post (SHOs, registrars and senior registrars) are also increasingly working in both hospital and community settings. The place in which a service is delivered is becoming less relevant as a basis for service organisation and staffing. A more relevant distinction is between primary and secondary care. The Joint Working Party on Medical Services for Children of the British Medical Association and the Department of Health (Ref. 24) has recently recommended a single staffing structure for 'consultant-led combined child health services' (i.e secondary care services), with staff working in both hospital and community settings.

61. The British Paediatric Association advises that:

'*Doctors working in the CMO grade should be able to contribute to the 'safety net' (emergency cover)*" (*Ref. 25*).

Analysis of advertisements for CMO posts in the British Medical Journal carried out by the BPA showed that between July 1990 and July 1991, 45% included acute on-call responsibilities, rising to 60% (of 222 advertisements) between July 1991 and July 1992. But many existing CMOs will require additional training to do this. Some will be unable to take on this role. Nevertheless, the expenditure represented by CMOs, together with that already committed to hospital-based staff, represents a significant resource which should be used to provide paediatric services in whatever setting they are needed. The need for experienced staff to cover the on-call rotas should be one factor which will be considered when deciding how this resource should be allocated. It is up to district health authorities (DHAs) as the main commissioning bodies to ensure that funds are channelled to the appropriate providers and that their work is properly co-ordinated.

(ii) Surgeons and anaesthetists

62. The special skills required of both surgeons and anaesthetists who care for children can be brought together, and maintained, if children requiring surgery are grouped into separate operating lists and the number of different surgeons and anaesthetists involved are minimised. Concentrating children into separate lists may also encourage a more child and family-centred approach amongst the whole surgical team, including operating theatre and recovery staff.

63. One consultant in each surgical specialty should be responsible for overseeing policies for the treatment of children within that specialty. The policies should include arrangements for emergency cover for children, to ensure that only staff with sufficient experience operate on children.

(iii) Nurses

64. RSCNs are an essential component in matching the special skills of staff who care for children to the needs of those children. There is no reason why it should cost more to employ RSCNs than Registered General Nurses (RGNs). However, RSCNs tend to be employed at higher grades at the moment because the children's element of their training has traditionally

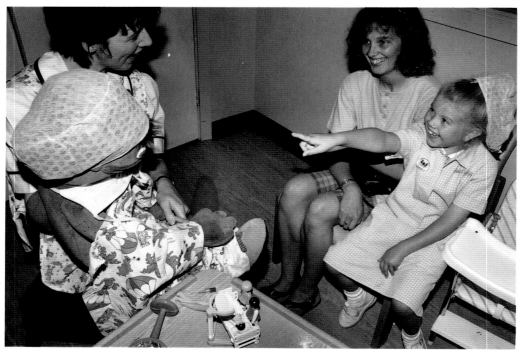

been obtained after their general training. This is changing with the advent of Project 2000, and the child training will in future be a primary qualification.

65. There are two important steps managers could take to make more effective use of their existing RSCNs:

— ensure that proper attention is given to the need for at least 2 RSCNs per shift when the rosters are being drawn up;

— ensure that RSCNs are primarily employed in children's services and not working as RGNs elsewhere in the hospital.

66. If more RSCNs are needed managers should:

— begin a policy of positive encouragement to attract newly qualified and existing RSCNs back to children's nursing. The number of sick children's nurses in training increased by 35% between 1988/89 and 1990/91 (Ref. 26). 'There are enough RSCNs in all age groups who are outside children's nursing, outside the NHS and not in employment to make it worth considering ways of bringing them back to sick children's nursing' (Ref. 13, page 166);

— increase the availability of post registration training. Some regional health authorities (RHAs) have top-sliced funds for this training as part of the policy of matching training expenditure more closely to the needs of the service (Ref. 27). RGNs who have at least 3 years experience of working with children can register as children's nurses by completing a 26 week course. However, a survey carried out in 1992 by the English National Board for Nursing, Midwifery and Health Visiting (ENB) found that over half of 174 health authorities or NHS trusts covered, had no strategy for secondment (Ref. 26).

67. Lack of a career structure for RSCNs may have caused some of them to move into other areas of nursing. The employment of a RSCN above ward sister level as part of the management focus recommended for children's services (page 12) should help to overcome this problem. It may also increase the status of RSCNs.

(iv) Play staff

68. All hospitals should employ qualified play staff. As well as organising play, play specialists should be a source of advice on the role of play, take the lead in developing play facilities and be involved in teaching other staff about play. They also have an important one-to-one role with the child, being a member of staff who is unlikely to cause the child pain and discomfort. The Department of Health has recommended that they should be a separately defined occupational group (Ref. 28).

69. The number of play staff needed in a particular hospital depends on the nature of the care provided, the ages of the children involved and the existence of complementary teaching staff. Teaching staff, employed by the local education authority, also work in some hospitals. They tend to work mainly with children aged 5 years and over.

Financing specially skilled staff

70. Many of the improvements suggested in this section can be made at little or no additional cost, because they involve reallocating or replacing existing staff. Some improvements will

involve transitional costs, such as re-training existing staff. In a few cases additional staff will be needed. Additional junior doctors may also be needed to meet the Department of Health's target of 83 working hours per week for those on call by April 1993, with the aim of reducing this to a maximum of 72 hours per week by 1994 and extending it to all junior doctors by 1996 (Ref. 29). If it is not possible to find the resources from other budget headings or efficiency improvements (such as those suggested later in this report) the viability of the service must be open to question. If there are insufficient junior doctors to provide in-patient care with full 'safety net' cover, services will need to be concentrated in larger units.

71. The breakdown of tasks between different groups of staff and the skills necessary for carrying them out are important issues in allocating the budget for staffing. There are moves to increase the role of nurse practitioners in children's services (e.g. in intensive care and in A&E departments) to release doctors for other duties. Similarly, health care assistants (working on wards under the supervision of nurses), clerical and housekeeping support staff and ancillary staff can release nurses for other duties. These moves should be encouraged as long as the staff receive training on the special needs of children and their families. Hospitals should regularly review the skill mix of their staff in relation to the needs and degree of dependency of children and families for whom they care. There is also a need for more research at national level into the effects of different skill mixes on the outcomes of care and ways in which hospitals can monitor this. The Audit Commission has already considered some of these issues in its reports on nursing (Refs. 11 and 30) and will be examining them further in its forthcoming study of medical staffing due for completion in 1994.

ENSURING ACCESS TO TERTIARY SERVICES

72. Children with relatively rare conditions like cancer or very low birthweight babies, should receive care at large tertiary centres because mortality rates are lower and the services can often be provided more efficiently as a result of economies of scale. But this does not always mean they will have to travel long distances. For example, at the Royal Liverpool Children's Hospital (Alder Hey), the consultant responsible for children with cystic fibrosis travels to local hospitals to undertake out-patient clinics. 'Shared care' between tertiary and secondary centres is possible for conditions such as cystic fibrosis and cancer, where the staff at the tertiary centre can advise, but the care is provided at the secondary centre. But it does require the responsibilities of the staff involved to be agreed and documented. Not all conditions which require tertiary care can be dealt with in this way. Intensive care for very low birthweight babies is a good example of a service which needs to be located at the tertiary centre.

73. Field (Ref. 16) concluded that units undertaking less than 500 intensive care days per year are not doing sufficient work to provide long term intensive care of babies who are most at risk. It implies an average of fewer than 1.5 babies receiving intensive care on any one day. Fewer than 30% of units are operating above this level *for all babies receiving intensive care* (Exhibit 8). Some units with very small numbers of intensive care days may be providing short term intensive care prior to transfer of the baby, but this is unlikely to account for more than 20 or 30 days per year. If all intensive care for newborn babies were concentrated at units doing about 5000 days at all levels of care (about 1,600 days would be intensive care - a level observed at some units), the total cost of providing this service could fall by about £3m nationally. Lack of available cots

Exhibit 8
ANNUAL NUMBERS OF INTENSIVE CARE DAYS IN A SAMPLE OF NEONATAL UNITS IN 3 REGIONS, 1991.
Fewer than 30% of the units undertaking intensive care do more than 500 days of intensive care per year.

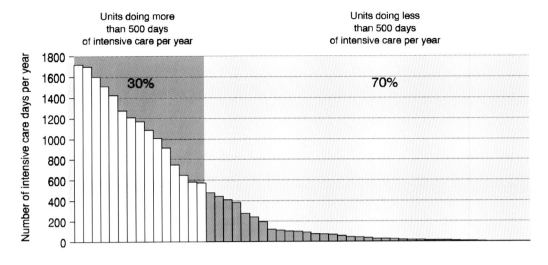

Note: *Intensive care is defined here as: continuous supervision by nursing and medical staff, including assisted ventilation.*

Source: *Trent, Northern and S E Thames regional surveys.*

at some tertiary units may be a problem, but this should only be transitory if the resources are transferred from units currently doing too little intensive care. In other countries such as Canada and the Netherlands, intensive care of newborn babies is concentrated in specific units. The House of Commons Select Committee on Health recently supported this line (Ref. 31) and the Clinical Standards Advisory Group is now examining the issue.

74. There will be some additional costs for the families involved in travelling to tertiary centres. Some families with low incomes will need assistance with their travel costs. The hospital travel cost scheme is already in place to meet these needs, but at the moment it does not include the costs of travel by parents (and siblings).

75. In assessing the overall cost and benefits of locating services at tertiary rather than secondary centres, the additional travel costs must be set alongside the benefits of lower mortality and lower costs to the NHS (releasing resources which can be used in other areas of care). It is important that the families involved and the community at large are aware of the issues and the evidence. The DHA as the main commissioning authority is responsible for determining where neonatal intensive care should be provided. DHAs should review, as a matter of urgency, taking account of the views of the families involved and the community as a whole, what arrangements they have in place to ensure that children have access to tertiary centres when necessary. Providing intensive care of newborn babies at tertiary centres does not necessarily mean only expanding existing centres. New centres can be set up with better accessibility, as long as they are able to undertake sufficient work.

76. The Department of Health, the Welsh Office and national organisations involved with other areas of tertiary care such as paediatric intensive care and emergency surgery on children, should initiate studies to establish when treatment at tertiary centres is justified on the grounds of both outcomes and costs and when it can be safely and effectively provided locally, before further decentralisation of these specialised services occurs.

3. Separate Facilities

THE PRINCIPLES

77. Even if staff working with children have the right skills, the needs of children and their families cannot be properly met without appropriate facilities. The physical environment of each part of a hospital should be appropriate to the ages of its users. In the case of children and young people up to 18 years it should include facilities for play, leisure and recreation. It should also be safe and secure. The need for special facilities for children cuts across all areas of hospital care including A&E departments, out-patient departments, in-patient wards, day-case wards and special units like intensive care. If such facilities are available, no children should receive care elsewhere in the hospital.

78. Special facilities for children should be separate from those provided for adults because of the wide differences in their needs. Separate facilities for adolescents are needed for the same reason. As well as being more appropriate, separate facilities are often more cost effective because the range of tasks undertaken by staff is more concentrated and there is less duplication of special equipment and materials.

79. Facilities for parents are equally important as parents are part of their child's care. There should be sufficient space so that parents can be with the child at all times, and in in-patient wards, parents need somewhere to sleep, make drinks, wash, and somewhere to sit quietly without interruption. All hospitals should have a room set aside for a family with a seriously ill or dying child.

THE PROBLEMS

80. There are four main problems:

— lack of separate facilities;

— insufficient use made of existing separate facilities;

— poor facilities for adolescents;

— lack of provision for parents.

LACK OF SEPARATE FACILITIES

81. Most hospitals treating children have separate children's wards (defined as having a separate nursing establishment as well as being physically separate), but separate out-patient and A&E facilities (reserved exclusively for children) are much rarer (Exhibit 9). Fifty five percent of out-patient departments and 43% of A&E departments in 174 health authorities and NHS trusts surveyed by the ENB in 1992 *'were caring for children in non-designated paediatric areas'* (Ref. 26). A&E facilities are particularly important because for many children this is their first, and only, contact with hospital and children comprise about a quarter of the patients who attend A&E departments (Ref. 1). Some hospitals, although not possessing a completely separate children's

Exhibit 9

AVAILABILITY OF SEPARATE FACILITIES FOR CHILDREN.

Many hospitals have separate children's wards, but separate out-patient and A&E departments are much rarer.

Hospital	In-patient Wards	Out-patient Department	Accident & Emergency Department
1	✓	✓	✓ (medical only)
2	✓	✓	✓
3	✓	✓	✓
4	✓	✓	✗
5	✓	✓	✗
6	✓	✓	✗
7	✓	✗	✗
8	✓	✗	✗

Source: Audit Commission surveys.

A&E department, do have a separate waiting area and sometimes a separate treatment room, but they are not always available for use.

INSUFFICIENT USE OF EXISTING FACILITIES

82. Even where separate facilities are available, they are not necessarily used for the care of all children. In the case of children's wards and out-patient departments, the problem seems to lie primarily in the surgical specialties, particularly ophthalmology and ENT. In these specialties, children frequently receive care in adult wards, despite the existence of children's wards (Exhibit 10).

83. Surgeons prefer to treat children in adult wards dedicated to their particular specialty because:

— they have less control over the use of beds in children's wards;

— some surgeons fear that the consequent reduction in use of their designated beds may threaten the viability of their specialty in the hospital;

— they perceive a need for nurses trained specifically to deal with the procedures carried out in their particular specialty. Over a quarter of 174 health authorities and NHS trusts surveyed in 1992 by the ENB were providing ENT and ophthalmic services without RSCNs (Ref. 26).

Exhibit 10

USE OF SEPARATE CHILDREN'S WARDS AND OUT-PATIENT DEPARTMENTS BY SURGEONS.

The lack of use is confined largely to Ophthalmic and ENT surgeons.

(a)   Children's wards.

Hospital	Paediatric/ General Surgery	Orthopaedics	ENT	Ophthalmology
1	✓	✓	✓	✓
2	✓	✓	✓	✓
3	✓	✓	✓	✓
4	✓	✓	✓	✗
5	✓	✓	✓	✗
6	✓	✓	✓	✗
7	✓	✓	✗	✓
8	✓	✓	✗	✗

(b)   Children's out-patient departments.

Hospital	Paediatric/ General Surgery	Orthopaedics	ENT	Ophthalmology
1	✓	✓	✓	✓
2	✓	✓	✓	✗
3	✓	✓	✓	✗
4	✓	✓	✓	✗
5	✓	✓	✗	✗
6	✓	✓	✗	✗

Source: Audit Commission surveys.

POOR FACILITIES FOR ADOLESCENTS

84. The needs of adolescents are very different from those of young children. The ward environment is particularly important. The need for privacy is much greater in adolescents than younger children. As well as having a range of suitable books and games in a recreation area, they need somewhere quiet where they can talk with their friends. Peer company is very important for adolescents. A different approach in the use of ward facilities is also needed. They should have access to the ward kitchen to make tea or coffee, and often do not need to be subject to the same restrictive rules which are necessary for younger children.

85. One survey of adolescents in a district general hospital found there was no policy for the placement of adolescents on wards (Ref. 32). Consequently, some were admitted to children's wards and others to adult wards. Adult wards are increasingly populated by elderly people and children's wards by babies and young children. There were important gaps in meeting the needs

31

of adolescents in both types of ward, particularly in relation to the lack of privacy, absence of peer group company and poor facilities. Only 1 out of 10 sites visited in the Audit Commission study had a separate ward for adolescents. Some hospitals did at least have separate areas for adolescents in children's wards.

LACK OF PROVISION FOR PARENTS

86. Although most hospitals provide some facilities for parents to stay overnight, few of them keep records of the number who do or the availability of accommodation in relation to demand. Data from one shows that in recent years there has been a considerable increase in the number of parents staying (Exhibit 11).

Exhibit 11
NUMBER OF PARENTS STAYING AS A PERCENTAGE OF THE NUMBER OF CHILD IN-PATIENTS.
There has been an increase in the proportion of children whose parents stay overnight.

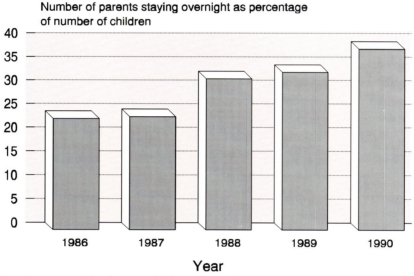

Source: *Data kept at ward level in one children's hospital.*

87. Despite the increased demand, there remain serious deficiencies in the provision of accommodation for parents. Firstly, it may be some distance from the ward. At one children's hospital, only 39% of parents staying were within 'dressing gown distance' of the ward. Secondly, a third of wards have no facilities for parents to wash or shower and lack other necessary facilities (Exhibit 12). Thirdly, few wards monitor parents' satisfaction with the facilities. Many of these deficiencies are worse for parents staying with their children in adult wards, rather than children's wards.

OVERCOMING THE PROBLEMS
PROVIDING SEPARATE FACILITIES

88. The main areas where separate facilities are lacking are A&E and out-patient departments. Hospitals should look urgently at how they can improve A&E facilities. A separate waiting area for children in A&E and a separate treatment room can make a very significant improvement and need not involve extensive capital expenditure.

Exhibit 12

FACILITIES FOR RESIDENT PARENTS – PERCENT OF WARDS WITH FACILITIES LISTED.

There are significant deficiencies in facilities for parents which are noticeably worse in adult wards.

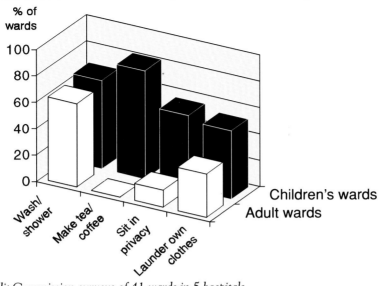

Source: Audit Commission surveys of 41 wards in 5 hospitals.

89. Although separate out-patient facilities are the best option (Box B), the use of general out-patient facilities by children can be much improved if the children are grouped together into separate clinics. The advantages of this are:

— appropriate staff and play facilities can be provided just for these sessions;

— flexibility in locating sessions is retained.

MAKING MAXIMUM USE OF EXISTING FACILITIES

90. The need to care for all children in separate facilities must be seen as paramount. All hospitals should strive to achieve this. Children should not be admitted to adult wards or share other facilities with adults where separate facilities already exist.

91. There is a need to counter the notion that the viability of a specialty and its importance depend on the number of beds within its control. The importance of a specialty depends on the number of patients treated and the nature of the care that is given. Beds are only one input to that care.

92. Surgeons' needs for nurses to be trained in their particular specialties can often be met with a short period of focussed in-house training. It is important that the care of children is supervised by RSCNs. They are as capable as general nurses of undertaking additional training in particular specialties and in any case receive specific training in nursing children.

Box B
NOTTINGHAM CITY HOSPITAL OUT-PATIENTS DEPARTMENT.

IMPROVING FACILITIES FOR ADOLESCENTS

93. More hospitals should provide separate facilities for adolescents such as those at Wexham Park Hospital, Slough and other hospitals (Ref. 33). The numbers of adolescents admitted under the care of paediatricians are increasing as survival rates for adolescents with chronic illness, such as cystic fibrosis and cancer, continue to improve. There are already large numbers of adolescents admitted under the care of surgeons (Exhibit 3, page 6). The average daily number of adolescent in-patients at one hospital was 16 (varying from a minimum of 2 to a maximum of 27 over a three month period (Ref. 34)), sufficient to justify a separate ward or area. There is also scope for an increased awareness of the needs of adolescents amongst staff who deal with them.

IMPROVING FACILITIES FOR PARENTS

94. All hospitals should provide somewhere for parents to stay overnight, wash, make tea or coffee and to sit in privacy. These should be as close as possible to the ward. Hospitals should make someone responsible for ensuring that everything works smoothly: a 'parents liaison officer'.

95. It is also important to monitor parents' satisfaction with the facilities. But sometimes well intentioned surveys turn into self-fulfilling prophesies because the questionnaires are poorly designed and given to parents in situations where they are unlikely to be critical. There is a need for national organisations to give a lead by producing questionnaires which have been proven by field testing. They can then be given to parents when they leave the hospital to allow them time for a more considered response.

4. Effective Treatments

96. The improvements in management, communications, staffing and facilities suggested in the previous chapters are interdependent. Clear policies for child and family-centred care are unlikely to work effectively without specially skilled staff and separate facilities. In most hospitals the changes which are necessary can be implemented at minimal additional cost. But many clinicians and managers will claim that the ideal service is a counsel of perfection, and in a health service where demand always outstrips supply, such quality will not be achieved without significant increases in expenditure.

97. This line of argument assumes that all hospital activity in relation to children is necessary and appropriate. But both assumptions are dubious. Are all treatments effective, and are all admissions to hospital necessary? These two questions are covered by this chapter and the next. They hold the key to ensuring that sufficient resources are available to take advantage of developments in the methods of care which meet the needs of children and their families more effectively.

THE PRINCIPLES

98. All hospitals should strive to ensure that the care and treatments they offer are effective. This means that they are achieving the desired improvement in the health and well being of children (the outcome) and that there are not alternative ways of doing this which offer less disruption and stress to the children and families involved or lower costs to the NHS. It is important that outcomes are monitored to ensure that effective care is provided consistently, to identify any particular shortcomings which can be remedied and to keep abreast of changing needs.

THE PROBLEMS

99. In common with many areas of health care, **the outcomes of treating and caring for children are not routinely monitored, making it difficult to say whether those treatments are effective.** This can be illustrated by means of two examples: the management of glue ear and intensive care for newborn babies.

POOR MANAGEMENT OF GLUE EAR

100. Glue ear (blockage of the middle ear with mucus) is a common condition in childhood. It often results in impaired hearing and can lead to delay in language development and learning of a child. It is not generally a painful condition unless the middle ear becomes infected, when it can be treated with antibiotics. But by far the most common approach to the problem of glue ear is to treat it surgically by: myringotomy (a small cut in the ear drum usually accompanied by the insertion of a small plastic tube - grommet), adenoidectomy (removal of the adenoids) or, less commonly, tonsillectomy (removal of the tonsils). The last two procedures are also used to treat conditions other than glue ear.

101. These three procedures account for almost all ENT surgery in children. They are often carried out in combination with each other. Comparisons of treatment rates of the individual procedures show wide variations from one district to another (Exhibit 13). They are also subject to wide variations in length of stay when performed in in-patient settings. The Audit Commission has shown in a previous report that there is considerable scope for nearly all myringotomies to be carried out on a day-case basis (Ref. 35).

Exhibit 13
ADMISSIONS (IN-PATIENTS AND DAY CASES) FOR MYRINGOTOMY AND TONSILLECTOMY IN 26 DHAS IN OXFORD AND EAST ANGLIAN REGIONS, 1990/91.
There is wide variation in treatment rates for these procedures.

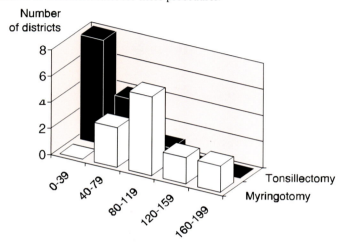

Admissions per 10,000 resident population

Source: Health Services Research Unit. London School of Hygiene and Tropical Medicine.

102. Over recent years the number of myringotomies has been growing. They are currently estimated to be costing about £30m per year in England and Wales (Ref. 36). Black has described this as an 'epidemic' which is not related to an increase in the underlying prevalence of glue ear (Ref. 37). He has also shown that much of this growth has taken place against a background of a decline in the number of tonsillectomies. Yet despite more than 19 randomised controlled trials recently reviewed, there still seems to be uncertainty about the appropriate indications for surgery for glue ear and a lack of routine monitoring of its implications on the well-being of the child (Ref. 36).

103. The significance of glue ear relates more to the disability which can result from a hearing loss, rather then the hearing loss itself. Also, the condition can improve spontaneously, avoiding the need for surgery. One study found that as many as 34% of ears did not contain mucus at the time of surgery (Ref. 38). Other studies have found that on average the improvement in hearing following myringotomy or adenoidectomy is small (Ref. 36). Some children do achieve significant improvements, but the studies have not identified their particular characteristics. Nevertheless the improvement may be short-lived as grommets often drop out, necessitating a repeat operation.

104. There are also negative effects of surgery which should be taken into account. Apart from the risk involved with having a general anaesthetic, grommet insertion can cause other long term ear problems (Ref. 36). Having grommets may also restrict a child's activity. Diving into water may be a problem because of the pressures it exerts on the ear drum. Some ENT surgeons recommend no swimming at all because of the risk of infection, but there is little evidence to support this (Ref. 36).

LACK OF OUTCOME MEASURES FOR INTENSIVE CARE OF NEWBORN BABIES

105. About 2% of newborn babies now receive intensive care, primarily because they are born prematurely. It is a service which has seen rapid growth over recent years (Exhibit 14) despite being very expensive (page 22). The growth has been due mainly to clinical and technological developments resulting in a better chance of survival for premature babies. The number of low birthweight babies being born as a result of multiple births has also increased due to more assisted conceptions.

Exhibit 14
NUMBER OF BABIES ADMITTED FOR INTENSIVE CARE IN NORTHERN RHA.
Since the early 1980s, the number of newborn babies receiving intensive care has grown rapidly.

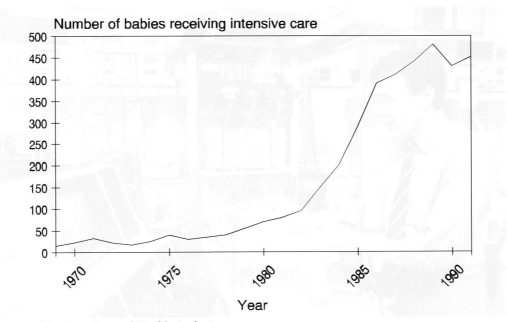

Source: Northern Regional Health Authority.

106. The benefit of these developments has been a substantial reduction in mortality rates for low birthweight babies over the past 20 years, but particularly for babies of less than 1500 grams at birth, where most of the deaths occur (Exhibit 15, overleaf). However, the degree to which surviving babies suffer disabilities, such as cerebral palsy and deficiencies of vision and hearing, and the effects of this on the quality of life of the baby and the family, are not routinely monitored. It is important that these effects are monitored so that doctors and parents can make informed decisions about the suitability of interventions for particular babies, and for medical audit.

Exhibit 15

NEONATAL MORTALITY RATES BY BIRTHWEIGHT. ENGLAND AND WALES, 1953 - 1989.

Mortality rates have declined rapidly in recent years, especially for babies weighing less than 1500 grams.

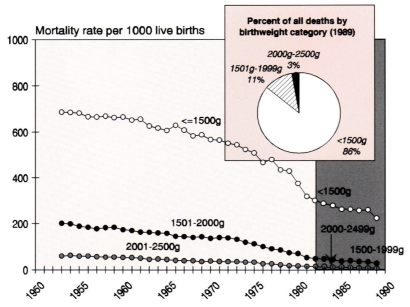

Source: Ref. 39 and OPCS.

OVERCOMING THE PROBLEMS

107. Outcome measurement has a major role to play in every hospital to ensure that the most effective services are being provided. But such measurement is difficult, expensive and time consuming, and it will not be possible initially to tackle all treatments. The management of glue ear and intensive care for newborn babies are good starting points because of the large numbers of children involved and the high costs of treatment (respectively).

IMPROVING THE MANAGEMENT OF GLUE EAR

108. Paediatricians and ENT surgeons should agree guidelines for the management of glue ear so that it is clear which children could benefit most from a medical approach and which from a surgical approach. The initial diagnosis of a child should include:

— an otoscopy (observation of the ear drum);

— an assessment using tympanometry (pressure testing of the ear drum to determine whether mucus is present);

— a hearing test to determine the extent of any hearing loss and that it is caused by glue ear;

— a speech and language assessment to determine the extent of any disability.

109. Only children with a significant bilateral hearing loss which is affecting their language and learning and which is clearly attributable to glue ear should be considered suitable for immediate surgery. Other children should be reassessed after 3-6 months to check whether the condition has improved. An assessment following surgery should also be carried out and subsequent problems recorded. The views of parents and teachers should be included in these

40

assessments. Parents sometimes see surgery as the answer if their child has repeated middle ear infections, but they should be made aware of the likely prognosis of the condition and the alternative treatments.

110. The incidence of 'dry taps' (the percentage of operations on individual ears which are found to have no mucus in them at the time of surgery) is an important measure of the quality of care. Children should be retested immediately prior to surgery so that this percentage is minimised. The assertion that dry taps are the result of nitrous oxide anaesthesia is not supported by the evidence (Ref. 36). Individual children should then be considered jointly by paediatricians and ENT surgeons as part of regular joint audits. Some GP fundholders, responsible for their own budgets for the management of glue ear, are already doing this monitoring themselves. If this monitoring could be co-ordinated nationally, it might enable the derivation of guidelines on the indications for surgery. Alternative treatments such as the use of hearing aids and autoinflation balloons (to drain the mucus away) should also be considered, although the latter is at the early stages of development and controlled trials are needed (Ref. 36).

OUTCOME MEASURES FOR INTENSIVE CARE OF NEWBORN BABIES

111. Intensive care for newborn babies has long term effects on the child and family which are even more significant than those for glue ear. It is also difficult to relate the outcome measures to the intervention. By the time outcome information is available – often several years after birth – procedures may have substantially changed as a result of technological developments. But outcome measures are an essential part of effective monitoring in neonatal units so that a unit can compare its performance over time and eventually – when measures of the severity of illness at birth have been developed – with other units. This information is also important for parents whose child may be admitted to the unit. A national data collection exercise is needed with all units collecting data in a nationally agreed format. The Audit Commission has developed a specification for such an exercise as part of this study, which it commends to the national bodies

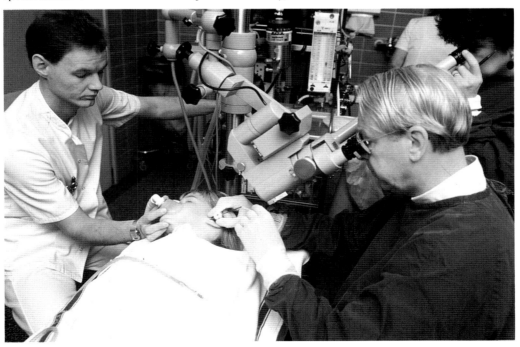

involved as an example. This is described in appendix 5. The Commission recommends that the relevant professional bodies, Department of Health and Welsh Office take steps to develop and implement such an exercise as soon as possible.

5. Appropriate Hospitalisation

THE PRINCIPLES

112. As well as striving to offer only effective treatments, it is necessary to ensure that they are delivered in the most appropriate setting, and in particular that hospital care is only used when it offers a therapeutic advantage over care at home. Hospitalisation ranges from in-patient care at one extreme, through day surgery and out-patient care at the other. The aim in delivering services should be to minimise the number of times a child needs to attend hospital and the length of time they stay on each occasion. Hospitals have an important role to play here, but much also depends on primary care. Good primary care can reduce the need for secondary care and provide support at home, enabling children to be discharged from hospital sooner.

BACKGROUND

113. The average length of stay of child in-patients has been falling in recent years in common with that of most in-patients in the NHS. But the number of admissions has been increasing. The fall in length of stay has occurred for children admitted in most specialties, but the growth in admissions has been confined to paediatrics (Exhibit 16, overleaf).

114. The fall in average length of stay has been due to:-

(i) **More day surgery**

Day surgery for children has expanded considerably during the past few years. (There is nevertheless, still wide variation from one hospital to another and the standards of care for children are sometimes poor (Ref. 40). In its study of day surgery the Audit Commission identified scope for further expansion of both adult and children's day surgery services (Ref. 35)).

(ii) **Changing nursing practices**

Nurses are now much more involved in teaching and supporting parents as prime care givers rather than providing the care directly themselves. This has enabled parents to become more competent and confident in caring for their ill child and the child to be discharged home earlier.

(iii) **More care at home**

Many new schemes have been set up to provide more care at home, involving children's nurses working in the community as a result of:

— **growth in demand for care at home** as many children who would have previously died are now surviving;

— **technological developments,** for example, in intravenous drug therapy and parenteral nutrition which have made these procedures suitable for application at home;

43

Exhibit 16
IN-PATIENT ADMISSION RATES FOR CHILDREN AGED 0 - 14 (1974 - 1990/91).
Falling length of stay has co-incided with a steady increase in the rate of admissions.

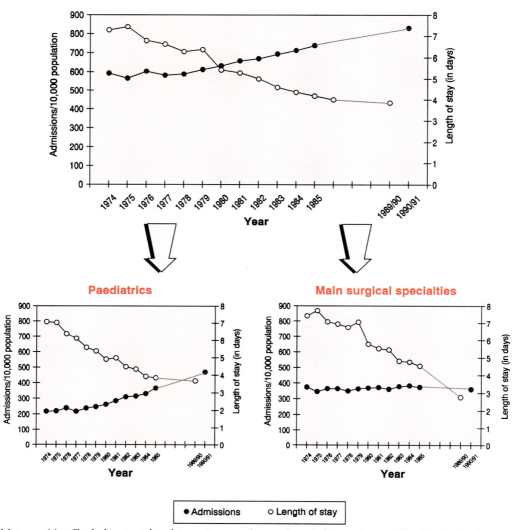

Note: (i)   *Excludes special and intensive care for newborn babies and normal healthy babies born in hospital.*
         (ii)   *Surgical specialties include: General Surgery, ENT, Trauma and Orthopaedics, Ophthalmology and Plastic Surgery.*
Sources: (i)   *1974 – 1980: Hospital In-patient Enquiry, England and Wales.*
         (ii)   *1981 – 1985 Hospital In-patient Enquiry, England only.*
         (iii) *1989 – 1991: Department of Health.*

— the realisation that home care is more cost effective than care in hospital.
Detailed studies which have attempted to match and compare children having home-based or hospital-based care have shown that home care is much more cost effective (Ref. 41). Other studies purely of the outcomes of care, have shown that they are at least as good (Ref. 42). There are additional costs for parents. But for many parents these are outweighed by the benefits for them and their child of being at home rather than in hospital (page 54).

115. Over 63% of the growth in admission rates in paediatrics observed by one author was due to asthma and related respiratory conditions (Ref. 43). This in turn is due to:

— an increase in the prevalence of asthma (Refs. 44 and 45);

— the availability of more effective treatments involving the use of nebulizers, which has increased the demand for hospital care.

116. Admission rates for special and intensive care for newborn babies (not shown in Exhibit 16) have been falling over recent years, but an average of about 10% of newborn babies still receive this care in special care baby units (Exhibit 17). The fall has partly been the result of a realisation that too many babies were being admitted for special care when they could receive equivalent care in post-natal wards; and partly a need to provide more cots for intensive care (Exhibit 14, page 39) which involves many more days per baby.

Exhibit 17
TRENDS IN ADMISSION RATES FOR SPECIAL AND INTENSIVE CARE FOR NEWBORN BABIES.
Admission rates for special and intensive care have been declining recently.

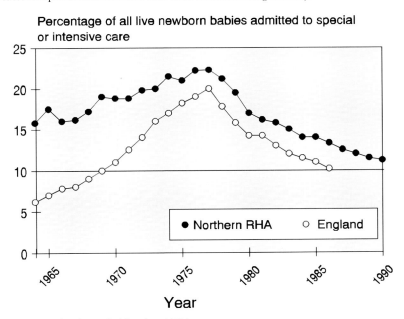

Note: Data for England unreliable after 1986.
Source: Northern RHA.

117. Data on admissions which are routinely collected by the NHS identify individual episodes of care, but not the patients receiving that care. It is therefore impossible to say whether the rising admission rates are due to more children being admitted to hospital or the same children being admitted more often. But an analysis using data from the Oxford Record Linkage Study shows (Table 2, overleaf) that between 1975 and 1985:

(i) the number of children who were admitted to hospital at least once in a year went up;

(ii) the number of multiple admissions (that is children admitted more than once in a year) also increased slightly; but,

45

(iii) the use of hospital beds went down by over a third in the age group 1-14, and it went up slightly for children aged under 1 year (Ref. 46).

In other words, assuming these results are representative of the whole country, most of the growth has been in first time, rather than multiple admissions. The fall in the use of beds shows that, despite the growth in the number of children admitted to hospital, they do tend to stay a shorter time overall except for those aged under 1 year. The latter reflects the growth in intensive care for newborn babies.

Table 2
CHANGES IN INDIVIDUAL ADMISSION RATES, ANNUAL EPISODES OF CARE AND LENGTH OF STAY. SIX DISTRICTS IN OXFORD REGION 1975 – 1985.
Most of the growth in admissions has been in first time, rather than multiple admissions. But the total days in hospital has fallen for 1 – 14 year olds.

	Number of children admitted at least once in a year per 1000 population	Episodes of care per child admitted	Length of stay per episode	Total days in hospital per year
Children aged under 1 year				
1975	199.4	1.15	7.47	9.13
1985	210.2	1.26	7.93	9.40*
% change (1975 – 1985)	+5%	+10%	+6%	+3%
Children aged 1-14 years				
1975	44.2	1.15	4.31	4.96
1985	55.6	1.20	2.54	3.09*
% change (1975 – 1985)	+26%	+4%	−41%	-38%

*   *1984 figures.*
Source: Unit of Clinical Epidemiology, University of Oxford.

THE PROBLEMS

118. There are three main problems:

— poor management of in-patient admissions;

— excessive lengths of stay in some hospitals;

— lack of home-care services.

POOR MANAGEMENT OF IN-PATIENT ADMISSIONS.

119. Admission rates of children vary widely from one area to another. The number of admissions per 'available bed' (throughput) in paediatrics, rises as the availability of beds decreases (Exhibit 18). This reflects lower average length of stay and/or a reduction in bed emptiness as

46

pressure on beds increases. Both responses raise the issue of whether beds are properly matched to demand. But, in looking at the performance of an individual hospital, there are some important problems with data on admissions and bed use in paediatrics:

— normal healthy babies are inconsistently recorded from one hospital to another and sometimes counted as admissions to paediatrics;

— admissions of all children to children's wards are sometimes attributed to paediatrics, when some children are under the care of surgeons and should be counted as admissions to the appropriate specialty;

— available beds in paediatrics is difficult to measure because beds in children's wards are not allocated to specific specialties and hospitals use different methods of calculating this figure (Ref. 47).

Exhibit 18
RELATIONSHIP OF THROUGHPUT AND BED AVAILABILITY IN PAEDIATRICS.
Throughput rises with fewer beds.

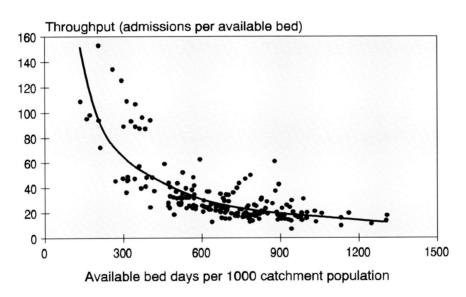

Source: Health Service Indicators 1989/90.

120. There is evidence that admission rates are higher for children in more deprived social groups (Ref. 48). This reflects: a poor environment, poor diet, lack of hygiene, higher rates of accidental and non-accidental injuries and inability of parents to cope. Also, clinical practices which affect admission rates vary according to the nature of the conditions being treated. Asthma and the need for special and intensive care for newborn babies account for over a quarter of admissions in paediatrics. As well as accounting for much of the recent growth in admissions (page 45), both are subject to wide variations in admission rates from one district to another.

(i) The treatment of asthma

121. Asthma is a very common condition amongst children – between 10% and 15% of children are affected. It is characterised by episodes of wheezing which vary in severity from mild

and inconvenient to severe and life threatening. The high admission rates for asthma in some areas (Exhibit 19) are due to:

— inexperienced junior doctors seeing children in A&E departments (page23);

— insufficient guidance for junior doctors in some A&E departments on when an admission is necessary;

— lack of facilities for the short term observation of children with asthma leading to automatic admission to a ward;

— lack of clarity of the respective roles of parents, GPs and hospitals in dealing with the disease.

The Audit Commission study has found very little evidence that clear written guidelines exist. The emphasis in those documents found at the study sites, where they existed, was on the medical management of the condition. Although one of the documents did have clear guidelines on indicators for admission, none of them had really tackled the interface with GPs, nor the role of continuing care.

Exhibit 19
ADMISSION FOR ASTHMA OF CHILDREN AGED 0-16 BY DHA OF RESIDENCE. (ENGLAND 1990/91).
The variation in admissions rates is at least fourfold.

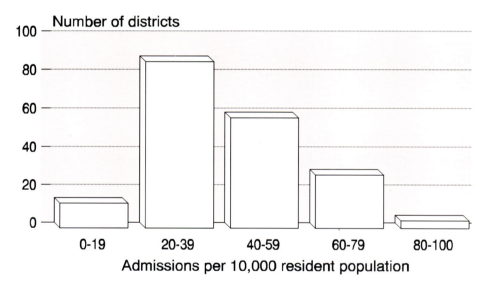

Source: Audit Commission analysis of national data.

(ii) Admissions of newborn babies for special and intensive care

122. Some hospitals admit as few as 4% of their newborn babies for special and intensive care. Others admit as many as 35% (Exhibit 20). Most of these admissions are for special care. Many babies presently admitted for special care, including most of those needing observation, phototherapy and blood glucose monitoring, could be nursed safely and more effectively on post-natal wards or in 'transitional care wards' - which are staffed to care for both mother and baby together, but do not require the intensity of staffing of a special care baby unit. High admission rates may simply be a consequence of spare capacity in special care baby units, but sometimes alternative facilities are not available or inappropriately staffed. If all hospitals reduced their admission rates to the levels achieved by those in the lower quartile (Exhibit 20), the total number of admissions to special care would fall nationally by about a third.

Exhibit 20
ADMISSIONS TO SPECIAL CARE AND INTENSIVE CARE AS A PROPORTION OF LIVE BIRTHS IN A SAMPLE OF 73 DHAS. VARIOUS YEARS FROM 1988 ONWARDS.
There is wide variation in the percentages of babies admitted to special and intensive care. Some hospitals admit fewer than 7%.

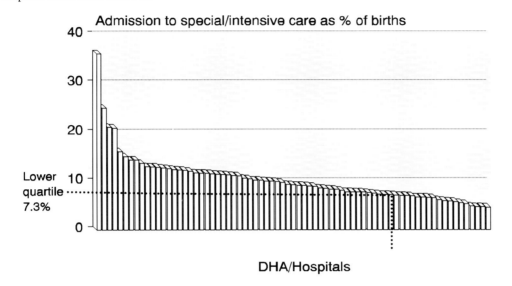

Source: Audit Commission surveys.

EXCESSIVE LENGTHS OF STAY IN SOME HOSPITALS

123. There is wide variation in the average length of stay in paediatrics, even after taking account of differences in medical conditions. In a sample of 200 district general hospitals in England, paediatric in-patient admissions were categorised into one of 475 diagnostic related groups (DRGs). The expected number of occupied bed days for each hospital was calculated by standardising its length of stay in each DRG against the average for the whole sample. The difference between the actual use of beds and that expected if lengths of stay were average, was considerable (Exhibit 21, overleaf). If all hospitals could match the length of stay achieved by hospitals in the lower quartile, occupied bed days in paediatrics would fall nationally by about 10%.

Exhibit 21
THE VARIATION IN BED USE AFTER ADJUSTING FOR DIFFERENCES IN THE NATURE OF CONDITIONS TREATED.

There is wide variation in bed use in paediatrics, even after taking account of differences in medical conditions.

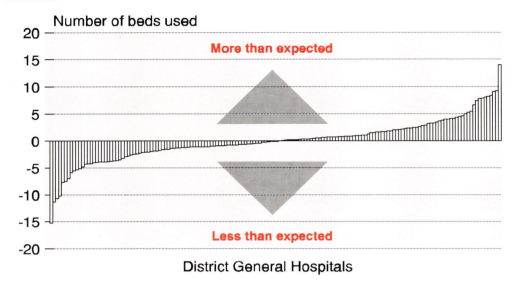

Source: Audit Commission data from 200 district general hospitals in England.

124. There are of course important reasons other than differences in the conditions treated which may explain the variation in length of stay: the severity of the illness, the social characteristics of the child involved and the availability of support services outside hospital are particularly important. One recent study of children with diabetes found that they stayed in hospital less if they were under the care of a paediatrician with a special interest in diabetes rather than the care of a general paediatricians (Ref. 49). The lower length of stay reported for this group was found to be significant irrespective of differences in the child's social background. Sometimes the problem of excessive length of stay is simply due to administrative delays: slow response to diagnostic tests or unnecessary tests, poor organisation of post discharge support services or unnecessarily awaiting a consultant's ward round before discharge can be agreed.

125. The responsibility of particular staff for discharge planning is sometimes poorly defined. In practice it is often left to a ward sister or senior nurse, but they may not have sufficient knowledge, nor the authority, to ensure that the needs are met. Their role in discharge planning may not be explicitly recognised in their job plans. In the case of many children coming to hospital for elective surgery, planning for discharge could take place before the date of admission.

LACK OF HOME CARE SERVICES

126. More care at home as a means of reducing hospitalisation can take one of two forms:-

(a) **Earlier discharge to primary care.** This includes routine post operative care and long term management of children with mild to moderate asthma.

(b) **Continuing secondary care at home.** This includes high technology therapies that require support from a hospital team and the care of terminally ill children such as those with AIDS.

The wide variation in length of stay in hospital for some conditions suggests that children could be discharged earlier, with follow-up by primary care teams or continuing care from specialised secondary care teams. An analysis of children who stayed in hospital more than seven days was carried out at one hospital. This showed that 11 children with fractures had taken up 291 days of care (an average of 26 days each) over a three month period. Some of this is routine care which could be carried out at home.

127. The number of reported schemes involving children's nurses working in the community has increased from 7 in 1980 to 28 in 1988 and currently stands at about 46 (Ref. 50), but many districts still do not have these services. Even where they do exist, often only one or two nurses are available in each district (Ref. 51).

OVERCOMING THE PROBLEMS
IMPROVING THE MANAGEMENT OF IN-PATIENT ADMISSIONS

128. It is important that the number of beds is properly matched to demand to avoid unnecessary use of resources. Decisions about the number of beds needed for children should be taken at the level of individual wards and for the hospital as a whole according to demand, and not according to notional allocations of these beds to individual specialties.

129. The problem of inconsistent recording of normal healthy babies born in hospital is a major one which can invalidate comparisons of admission rates between hospitals. The Department of Health and the Welsh Office should take steps to reduce this by, for example, making normal healthy babies born in hospital a separate 'specialty'. A consistent method for measuring bed availability and occupancy is also needed to enable comparisons between hospitals at national level. The problem of allocating beds to specialties would be avoided if both bed availability and occupancy were ward-based rather than specialty-based statistics.

130. Effective management of in-patient admissions for specific conditions is assisted by written guidelines which are agreed between all the staff involved, including GPs. These should be reviewed as part of joint clinical audits. This is particularly important when junior hospital medical staff are constantly changing. It is also important to ensure that all staff involved know that agreements on best practice are in place and that they can obtain copies quickly should they need to refer to them.

131. The guidelines could be extended to cover the complete management of the condition, out-patient attendances and long-term care as well as in-patient care. GP fundholders are increasingly seeking closer links with hospital consultants through the mechanism of their contracts for non-emergency services which include the need for regular out-patient reviews. All GPs should be seeking similar links at local level. Many GPs are now actively involved in the treatment of some conditions, such as asthma in children, by holding regular review clinics themselves. This is partly a result of the growth in the number of practice nurses who assist with these clinics, and the provision of separate funding for this work.

132. There are several key areas which should also be addressed:-

— **Employment of experienced medical staff in A&E and better training for existing staff.**
In one hospital admissions fell from 86% of A&E attendances for asthma, to 56% as a result of a training programme for junior doctors (Ref. 45).

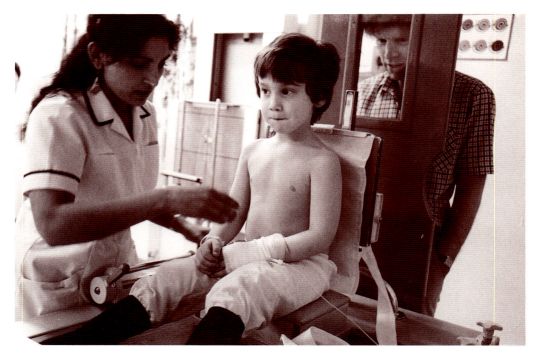

— **GPs' access to emergency consultations.** GPs should have access by telephone to experienced medical staff for consultations, which may in some cases obviate the need to send the patient to the ward.

— **Short-term observation facilities.** Hospitals should have facilities to observe children for up to 8 hours without the need for automatic admissions.

— **Health promotion and education.** All parts of the NHS should seek to improve the ability of parents to cope with their children's needs more effectively and thereby avoid accidents and disease. The provision of simple information in hospitals on how to avoid accidents in the home can reduce attendances at A&E departments and subsequent admissions.

REDUCING IN-PATIENT STAYS.

133. All hospitals should regularly review their length of stay profiles (the number of children staying for different lengths of time) for individual specialties and conditions, and investigate the reasons for some of the long stays with the clinicians involved. Appropriate lengths of stay should be part of the recommended guidelines for the management of particular conditions. The BPA recommends that a length of stay in excess of 3 days for asthma is a good indicator of poorly organised services and lack of involvement of primary care (Ref. 52). For conditions which are relatively rare, but not rare enough to warrant treatment at a tertiary centre - like diabetes, all the children involved should be under the care of one consultant who can develop a special expertise in that condition. This not only reduces length of stay, but has important benefits in improving overall management of the condition (Ref. 53).

134. Administrative delays in discharge can often be overcome by improved procedures, e.g. giving children and parents the results of tests after discharge if their stay in hospital is no longer necessary for medical reasons, consultants delegating the responsibility for discharge to junior staff or carrying out more frequent ward rounds (Ref. 54). A named discharge co-ordinator should be allocated to each child. This may be the nurse responsible for their care on the ward, or it may be someone whose sole responsibility is discharge planning. They should play a major role in communicating with services outside the hospital, particularly the GP, and ensuring that families are given written information to back-up oral explanations about continuing care when they leave the hospital (Ref. 55). Delay in informing the GP of discharge is a common problem. Many hospitals are now using facsimile machines to ensure GPs receive timely discharge summaries.

135. All 4 hospitals visited in North America as part of the Audit Commission study had central departments of discharge planning, It may cost more to employ these staff but their costs can be offset by quicker discharge and reduced administrative tasks for nurses.

PROVIDING MORE CARE AT HOME

136. The value of home care nursing to children and families is well illustrated from a survey of families of children with chronic illness (Box C overleaf). As well as reducing hospital stay, some nurses working with children at home have gone a stage further and begun to reduce hospital admissions by:

— providing **long-term support at home** and a 24-hour contact in an emergency. For less common conditions, like cystic fibrosis, the nurse can provide better guidance than many GPs based on greater experience. Home care nurses can also provide essential support to a family with a terminally ill child. But it is important that close links are maintained between all the staff involved in long-term support so that the role of each is clear to all concerned;

— taking **referrals directly from consultants** for some relatively minor conditions in children like constipation and gastroenteritis.

137. There is a need for more teams of RSCNs who can provide secondary care at home. Better use can also be made of existing primary care services. Both require careful planning. Teams providing secondary care at home need to have very close links with the hospital and GP. Some districts have combined child health services spanning both hospital and community settings (Ref. 23 and appendix 2) and home care would be part of these. But in many districts, hospital and community services are managed separately. In these districts whether home care teams should be managed as part of the hospital or community health services depends on local circumstances such as: the geography of the area, existing managerial structures and personal relationships between staff. Whichever management structure is adopted for secondary level home care services, clear lines of managerial and clinical responsibility are essential.

Box C
THE VALUE OF HOME CARE TEAMS.

> The results of a survey of 48 families of chronically ill children carried out as part of the Audit Commission study showed that home care nurses can:
>
> — reduce the amount of time some children need to stay in hospital;
>
> — present information in a more considered, calmer atmosphere, re-enforcing what they have already learnt in hospital;
> *'You are confused, you rush into the hospital, you sit awake overnight: tired and worried. And then you are bombarded with information' (Parent surveyed).*
>
> — help children and parents to come to terms with the diagnosis, to cope with the illness and give them confidence to provide day-to-day care;
> *'I was terrified of doing somthing wrong and could never have come out of hospital without the paediatric community nurse' (Parent surveyed).*
>
> — reduce the number of unnecessary hospital admissions.
>
> — provide a vital link with primary care teams and schools.
>
> This work has now been taken forward by Caring for Children in the Health Services to explore the links with primary care. A report is due to be published in February 1993.

138. Providing more home care will inevitably involve transitional costs, but in the longer term it should be possible to fund it from a reallocation of existing resources. The home care team which covers Nottingham City and University Hospitals is one of the largest and best established in this country (Ref. 56). Between 1989 and 1991 the number of beds in the children's wards at the two hospitals have been reduced from 205 to 193 (a fall of 6%) – partly as a result of the work of the team – and the resources released have been used to expand the home care service.

139. It is possible in many hospitals to find savings from existing services to fund home care. For example, there are several possibilities within the nursing budget itself (Ref. 11):

— reducing unnecessarily long overlapping shifts;

— reallocating clerical and housekeeping duties to non-nursing staff;

— reducing nurse management costs by reducing the number of separate management layers.

140. In the Audit Commission survey of families with chronically ill children, most families spoke very highly of the benefits they had received from home care services. The possibility of the families themselves incurring a greater burden of care was not identified as an issue. But for families with chronically ill, terminally ill or handicapped children there is a need for respite care which can take place in a variety of settings, including the hospital or home, depending on the needs of individual families. Studies are needed which compare the costs of alternative types of care received by similar patients. The few studies which have been carried out on this basis do suggest substantial cost benefits, but most of them are based on experience in other countries. There is a need for similar studies in the UK.

6. Strategic Commissioning

THE PRINCIPLES

141. Efficient and effective services for sick children depend as much on having a clear and consistent strategy for commissioning services as having a strategy for delivering them. DHAs are the main commissioning authorities. Their role is to set the framework in which providers operate. In particular, they maintain a vital link between several providers who may be delivering services in the same district. It is the role of the DHA to ensure that a comprehensive range of effective services are provided and properly co-ordinated.

142. The Audit Commission will be publishing a separate report on the commissioning role of DHAs within the next few months. Many of the issues discussed in this chapter will be taken up in more detail in that report.

THE PROBLEMS

143. There are four main problems:

— lack of commissioning strategies;

— poor specification of services in contracts;

— inadequate links between commissioning authorities and providers;

— lack of attention to the need for change.

LACK OF COMMISSIONING STRATEGIES

144. DHAs became responsible for commissioning services in April 1991. The task is therefore a relatively new one. It is not surprising to find that very few DHAs have clear strategies for children's services, but it is surprising to find that very few have firm plans for developing a strategy. The assessment of needs is still very much in its infancy. Few DHAs can clearly relate the services they provide to the needs of their populations. Some DHAs do not even classify children's services as a separate entity but group them with adult services, particularly in contracts for surgery.

145. An important underlying problem is the lack of information on which strategies can be based. Broad activity data, primarily used for funding and budgetary purposes, is insufficiently detailed and often focuses primarily on hospital care. At the other extreme, many hospitals are now developing detailed medical audit information systems independent of existing hospital information systems. The level of information needed for strategies and contracting is between these two extremes, but few hospitals are developing information systems at this level.

POOR SPECIFICATION OF SERVICES IN CONTRACTS

146. The lack of a strategy, lack of evidence on underlying needs and poor information on services are the main reasons for the poor specification of services in contracts. This includes a lack of clarity on when tertiary care is appropriate and lack of attention to the quality of services.

147. Some children have conditions which are relatively rare and which may require the skills of specialist staff available only at tertiary centres (page 21). But some DHAs do not specify clear ground rules for when a tertiary referral is warranted and do not place contracts with the tertiary centres. Instead, they rely on extra contractual referrals as a means of gaining access to these services. This leaves the decision to refer largely in the hands of providers. It also means that the workload and financing of the tertiary centre is uncertain. In the absence of clear plans, the viability of the tertiary services may be threatened.

148. Some DHAs have general quality specifications for children's services, including waiting times for appointments and for treatments in clinics. But the child-focussed quality specifications discussed in this report are rare. Although many DHAs express support for the NAWCH Charter in their contracts, there is often no assessment of the extent to which its standards are currently being met, nor plans to monitor this in the future. Yet there is little doubt, as this report has shown, that many of these standards are not being met.

INADEQUATE LINKS BETWEEN COMMISSIONING AUTHORITIES AND PROVIDERS

149. Co-ordination of services is important from the children's and families' points of view so that they understand the role of each service, know how to gain access to it and do not receive inconsistent or conflicting information. It also helps to avoid wasteful duplication and inefficient use of resources. Yet DHAs often have only general statements in their strategies or contracts in favour of 'integrated' services or the need for 'seamless' care (appendix 2). They frequently do not identify the meanings of these terms nor make it clear how they should be achieved.

150. Some DHAs are in a weak position to enforce the standards they have agreed in the contracts because they have failed to specify the information they will need to do so, to agree rights of access to the facilities and to monitor services.

LACK OF ATTENTION TO THE NEED FOR CHANGE

151. Few DHAs have an action plan for children's services. Even where specific areas for change are mentioned in strategies or contracts, the precise objectives are often inadequately specified (e.g. 'improve facilities for parents'), poorly monitored (no specific report back date given nor clear guidelines on the form that report should take) or poorly enforced (targets set for the next contract may not be reviewed when the new contract is being negotiated).

OVERCOMING THE PROBLEMS
DEVELOPING A STRATEGY

152. All DHAs should recognise that services for children require a separate strategy because the health care needs of children and their families are very different from those of adults. Services provided according to the structure of hospital specialties and departments do not necessarily correspond to these specific needs. A key principle in developing a needs-based strategy is to document the contribution of each component of the service to meeting the needs. This concentrates attention on the 'outputs' of the service.

153. Needs assessment is far too great a task to be tackled in sufficient detail for all children's services in a short time scale. DHAs should focus initially on key areas which involve large numbers of children or expensive services such as: chronic illness, care of the newborn and ENT surgery for children. In some areas Child Development Computer Systems may provide a useful database for looking at the needs for health care if they have been fully used and include details of treatments as well as regular health checks.

154. Information in general is an area which is in need of improvement. DHAs could make a start with this task by ensuring that they are aware of, and able to utilise, the information sources available within the hospitals with which they work, including those for medical audit. The Audit Commission is about to be begin a new project on information technology needs and management which is due to report in 1994.

IMPROVING THE SPECIFICATION OF SERVICES

155. If needs are related to specific groups of children and their families it should be possible to combine necessary services for each group into a single contract. This does not mean that there should be specific fully-fledged contracts for every treatment or care group. Oxfordshire DHA has developed an approach to contracting which is based on four separate levels:

(i)   all services;

(ii)   children's services as a whole;

(iii) individual specialties;

(iv)   individual treatments.

The idea is that more detailed aspects of the service are taken up as required (Exhibit 22, overleaf).

156. Commissioning authorities should not try to specify every detail of the quality of care. But they should, *at the very least*, ensure that each hospital has a written policy for the care of sick children, that it covers the principles set out in the Department of Health's guidelines (Ref. 4) and that appropriate procedures are in place for its implementation and monitoring. They can then select a small number of key indicators (such as those suggested in appendix 3) for monitoring. They should also ensure that the information they receive is sufficiently detailed to monitor the standards they have set and inspect facilities as much as necessary.

BETTER LINKS WITH PROVIDERS

157. Difficulty in co-ordinating services between providers is compounded where contracts are based on individual specialties and departments rather than the needs of specific groups, such as children with asthma or diabetes or children who have undergone major surgery. In some of the more complex cases, e.g. a child with cystic fibrosis, several providers may be involved (Exhibit 23). These children will need a 'key worker' designated to ensure that co-ordination takes place with agencies outside the NHS as well as those within it. Bringing the majority of these services under one management structure may also help, but is not possible in every district because of constraints outside the child health services (appendix 2). Effective co-ordination should still be possible. Operational co-ordination could be improved if the commissioning authority could contract with one of the providers to oversee the total budget for the service, sub-contracting as necessary, within clear ground rules, to other providers (the Welsh Office already recommend this

Exhibit 22
LEVELS OF SERVICE SPECIFICATIONS.
As the service needed becomes more specific, more detailed service specifications can be added.

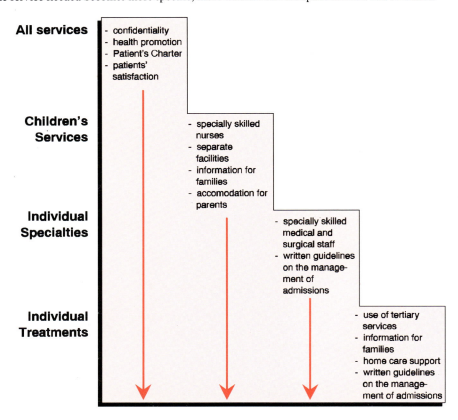

All services
- confidentiality
- health promotion
- Patient's Charter
- patients' satisfaction

Children's Services
- specially skilled nurses
- separate facilities
- information for families
- accomodation for parents

Individual Specialties
- specially skilled medical and surgical staff
- written guidelines on the management of admissions

Individual Treatments
- use of tertiary services
- information for families
- home care support
- written guidelines on the management of admissions

Source: Audit Commission.

Exhibit 23
THE COMPLEX JIGSAW OF SERVICE NEEDS FOR A CHILD AND FAMILY WITH CYSTIC FIBROSIS.
Who is responsible for co-ordination?

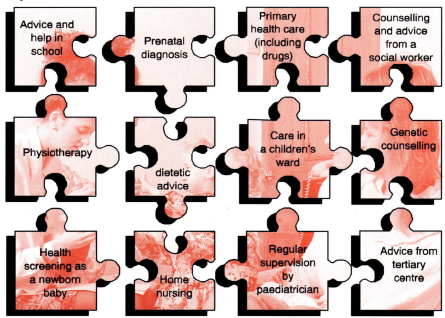

Advice and help in school

Prenatal diagnosis

Primary health care (including drugs)

Counselling and advice from a social worker

Physiotherapy

dietetic advice

Care in a children's ward

Genetic counselling

Health screening as a newborn baby

Home nursing

Regular supervision by paediatrician

Advice from tertiary centre

Source: Audit Commission.

– Ref. 57). Otherwise the commissioning authority itself will need to adopt a more active role in ensuring that co-ordination takes place between services for which they have separate contracts (Exhibit 24).

Exhibit 24
THE RELATIONSHIP BETWEEN COMMISSIONING AUTHORITIES AND PROVIDERS.
DHAs commissioning care from more than one provider will need to play an active role in co-ordinating services unless they contract this role to one of the providers.

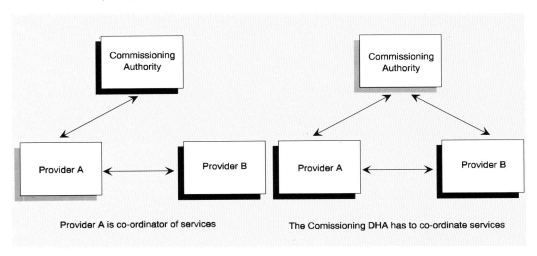

Source: Audit Commission.

158. The approach to contracting for a specific quality of care adopted by Oxfordshire DHA, can be applied to the problem of co-ordination. Where necessary, contracts can overlap with each other to ensure that the responsibilities of different providers are clear and are agreed by all involved. The contracts can be used at the level of individual specialties, as well as providing a means of dealing with the more complex cases of co-ordination for children with chronic illness or special needs. The method also provides a simple, but effective means for commissioning authorities to clarify responsibilities. Clear responsibilities, including named individuals, are an essential element of effective co-ordination.

ADDRESSING THE NEED FOR CHANGE

159. Commissioning authorities should be questioning the need for existing services to ensure that only effective treatments are offered and that services are responsive to changes in the underlying needs and methods of service delivery. Commissioning authorities are the main catalysts for change in the NHS because they control the funds used to provide the services.

160. All Commissioning authorities should have an action plan in place to improve services, which is regularly reviewed. The action plan should be based on an analysis of the current strengths and weaknesses of services according to the needs of users and the overall effectiveness of the services. Appropriate actions can then be specified with clear responsibilities for their implementation and a definite date when progress will be monitored. This should involve close liaison with the providers perhaps through a joint purchaser/provider working group. Much of

the expertise on existing services in a district lies with providers and commissioning authorities should rely on their providers as the first source of advice.

The Next Steps

161. The Audit Commission's auditors are already undertaking audits of services for sick children in hospitals in England and Wales. These, together with this report should form the basis of local strategies to improve services. The two key elements of these strategies are:

— establishment of a senior management focus for children's services;

— developing a written operational policy for children's services based on existing national principles and standards, and the good practice guidelines discussed in this report.

Strategies should be comprehensive in two respects:

— **the principles they embrace.** Including the effectiveness, efficiency and management issues, as well as the well established principles for the quality of care;

— **their scope within the hospital**. They should include all departments and services which work with children, and apply a consistent approach in each.

162. Implementation of the strategy is mainly the responsibility of hospitals as providers and DHAs as commissioning authorities, but the government departments and professional and voluntary bodies also have a role to play.

HOSPITALS

163. The changes needed in children's services in some hospitals will require a major shift in the attitudes and approach of management. It is essential that the reasons for this are discussed with staff at the earliest opportunity. The management of change requires:

— an assessment of the current position;

— a clear vision of the ideal service against which to judge the need for change;

— firm objectives and responsibilities for all staff who will be the prime agents of change and a timetable for the achievement of the objectives;

— measurable indicators against which progress can be monitored.

164. Services for children are at the forefront of 'care group' management in the NHS. This means a management approach based on the outputs of the services (like child and family-centred care), rather than the inputs (such as wards and specialties). The benefits of this approach are that the needs of users are paramount and services are more responsive to changes in these needs. If hospitals can make a success of care group management based on children's services, there are likely to be important lessons for the management of services for other care groups.

COMMISSIONING AUTHORITIES

165. Commissioning authorities should by now have strategies in place for the care of sick children. These should be broader than those for individual hospitals, and encompass the issue

of co-ordination between different providers. Commissioning authorities are also an important catalyst for change because they provide the funds within which hospitals must work. Where service improvements require shifts in resources between separate hospital units or trusts, or between hospitals and community services, commissioning authorities should facilitate these shifts.

166. Commissioning authorities should state clearly in their contracts which services can be appropriately provided at district general hospitals and which should be the responsibility of tertiary centres. They are also responsible for ensuring that these ground rules are followed.

THE DEPARTMENT OF HEALTH AND THE WELSH OFFICE

167. Both have played a major role alongside professional and voluntary bodies in clarifying the principles and standards according to which children should receive care in hospital. Their role now is to reinforce the importance of existing policies and to extend them in the light of this report. In particular, the government departments should:

— provide guidelines on which services should be provided at secondary centres and which at tertiary centres;

— address the problem of inadequate data at national level, particularly the confusion over counting normal healthy babies born in hospital as admissions, and the inconsistency in measures of bed availability and usage;

— set in train a much more rigourous approach to measuring the outcomes of health care. A start could be made using the guidelines for glue ear and intensive care for newborn babies set out in this report.

PROFESSIONAL AND VOLUNTARY BODIES

168. Many professional and voluntary bodies are involved with children's services. They will, no doubt, continue to campaign for high quality services and to offer advice and information on good practice, as they have done for many years. The BPA is already involved in producing outcome measures for child health (Ref. 52). The professional bodies could also extend the guidelines they offer to cover some of the detailed management issues highlighted in this report, for example, admissions for conditions such as asthma and professional involvement in home care. They could also offer more advice and 'blue print' questionnaires for monitoring children's and families' views of services. It is in everyone's interest that much more attention is given to measuring the effectiveness of health care and making health care practices more responsive to change. The professional bodies are well placed to take a leading role in these areas.

References

1   British Paediatric Association, British Association of Paediatric Surgeons and Casualty Surgeons Association (1988). *Joint Statement on Children's Attendances at Accident and Emergency Departments*.

2   Report of the Platt Committee (1959). *The Welfare of Children in Hospital*. HMSO.

3   Report of the Committee on Child Health Services (1976). *Fit for the Future*. HMSO.

4   Department of Health (1991). *Welfare of Children and Young People in Hospital*. HMSO.

5   J Robertson (1958). *Young Children in Hospital*. Tavistock Publications.

6   Department of Health (1991). *The Patient's Charter*.

7   Audit Commission for Local Authorities and the National Health Service in England and Wales (1992). *Minding the Quality: A Consultation Document on the Role of the Audit Commission in Quality Assurance in Health Care*.

8   Robin Dowie (1992). *Patterns of Hospital Medical Staffing: Overview*. British Post Graduate Medical Federation.

9   National Association for the Welfare of Children in Hospital (1990). *Quality Review: Setting Standards for Children in Health Care*.

10 National Association for the Welfare of Children in Hospital (1984). *The NAWCH Charter*.

11 Audit Commission for Local Authorities and the National Health Service in England and Wales (1991). *The Virtue of Patients: Making the Best Use of Ward Nursing Resources*. HMSO.

12 E A Campling, H B Devlin and J N Lunn (1989). *The Report of the National Confidential Enquiry into Perioperative Deaths*.

13 Rosemary Hutt (1983). *Sick Children's Nurses: a Study for the Department of Health and Social Security of the Career Patterns of RSCNs*. Institute of Manpower Studies, University of Sussex.

14 Play in Hospital Liaison Committee (1990). *Quality Management for Children: Play in Hospital*. National Association for the Welfare of Children in Hospital.

15 C A Stiller (1988). Centralisation of Treatment and Survival Rates for Cancer. *Archives of Disease in Childhood*, volume 63, pages 23 - 30.

16 D Field, S Hodges, E Mason, P Burton (1991). Survival and Place of Treatment after Premature Delivery. *Archives of Disease in Childhood*, Volume 66, pages 408 - 411.

17 N Panet, J L Kiely, S Wallenstein, M Marcus, J Pakter, M Susser (1982). Newborn Intensive Care and Neonatal Mortality in Low-birthweight Infants. *New England Journal of Medicine*, volume 307, pages 149 - 155.

18   S P Verloove-Vanhorick, R A Verwey, M C A Ebeling, R Brand, J H Ruys (1988). Mortality in Very Pre-term and Low Birthweight Infants According to Place of Delivery and Level of Care. *Pediatrics*, volume 81, pages 404 - 411.

19   Report of Working Group of the British Association of Perinatal Medicine and Neonatal Nurses Association on Categories of Babies Requiring Neonatal Care (1992). *Archives of Disease in Childhood*, volume 67, pages 866 - 869.

20   R Fordham (1992). Cost of Neonatal Care Across a Regional Health Authority. *Journal of Public Health Medicine*, volume 14, number 2, pages 127 -130.

21   M M Pollack, S R Alexander, Nancy Clarke, U E Ruttimann, Helen M Tesselaar, Antoinet C Bachulis (1991). Improved Outcomes for Tertiary Center Pediatric Intensive Care: A Statewide Comparison of Tertiary and Nontertiary Care Facilities. *Critical Care Medicine*, volume 19, number 2, pages 150 -159.

22   J D Atwell and P M Spargo (1992). The Provision of Safe Surgery for Children. *Archives of Disease in Childhood*, volume 67, pages 345 - 349.

23   British Paediatric Association (1991). *Towards a Combined Child Health Service*.

24   Report of The Joint Working Party on Medical Services for Children (1992). Conference of Medical Royal Colleges, British Medical Association and Department of Health.

25   British Paediatric Association (1991). *Paediatric Medical Staffing in the 1990s*.

26   English National Board for Nursing, Midwifery and Health Visiting (1992). *A Survey to Identify Progress Made Towards Meeting the Requirements of ENB Circular 1988/53/RMHLV - Supervision of Students Gaining Nursing Experience in Children's Wards*.

27   Department of Health (1989). *Working for Patients. Education and Training*. Working Paper 10. HMSO.

28   Department of Health (1992). *Hospital Play Staff*. Executive Letter EL(92)42.

29   Department of Health (1992). *'Dr Mawhinney hails real achievement in reducing junior doctors hours'*. Press Release, H92/365.

30   Audit Commission for Local Authorities and the National Health Service in England and Wales (1992). *Caring Systems: A Handbook for Managers of Nursing and Project Managers*. HMSO.

31   House of Commons Health Committee (1992). *Report on Maternity Services*. HMSO.

32   Susan M Burr (1990). *Adolescents and the Ward Environment*. Dissertation for degree of MA, Brunel University.

33   National Association for the Welfare of Children in Hospital (1990). *Setting Standards for Adolescents in Hospital*. Quality Review Series .

34   Majorie Gillies and W L Parry-Jones. (1992). *Adolescents in a Children's Hospital*. Department of Child and Adolescent Psychiatry. University of Glasgow.

35 Audit Commission for Local Authorities and the National Health Service in England and Wales (1990). *A Short Cut to Better Services: Day Surgery in England and Wales*. HMSO.

36 School of Public Health, University of Leeds, Centre for Health Economics, University of York and Royal College of Physicians (1992). The Treatment of Glue Ear in Children. *Effective Health Care*, number 4, November.

37 N Black (1985). Geographical Variations in Use of Surgery for Glue Ear. *Journal of the Royal Society of Medicine*, volume 78, August, pages 641 - 648.

38 N A Black, C F Sanderson, A P Freeland, M P Vessey (1990). A Randomised Controlled Trial of Surgery for Glue Ear. *British Medical Journal*, volume 300, pages 1551 - 1556.

39 Alison McFarlane and Miranda Mugford (1984). *Birth Counts: Statistics of Pregnancy and Childbirth*. HMSO

40 Caring for Children in the Health Services (1991). *Just for the Day: Children Admitted to Hospital for Day Treatment*. National Association for the Welfare of Children in Hospital.

41 T M Chamberlain, M E Lehman, M J Groh, W P Munroe and T P Reinders. (1988). Cost Analysis of a Home Intravenous Antibiotic Programme. *American Journal of Hospital Pharmacy*, volume 45, number 2, pages 2341 - 2345 .

42 M A Donati, G Guenette, H Auerbach (1987). Prospective Controlled Study of Home and Hospital Therapy of Cystic Fibrosis Pulmonary Disease. *Journal of Pediatrics*, volume 11, number 1, pages 28 - 33.

43 Alison M Hill (1989). Trends in Paediatric Medical Admissions. *British Medical Journal*, 3 June, volume 298, page 1479 - 1483.

44 David P Strachan, H Ross Anderson (1992). Trends in Hospital Admission Rates for Asthma in Children. *British Medical Journal*, 28 March, volume 304, pages 819 - 820.

45 G J Connet, C Wards, E Wooler, W Lenney (1992). *Strategies to Reduce Hospital Admissions for Acute Asthma*. In press.

46 J Henderson and M Goldacre (1991). Time Spent in Hospital by Children: Trends in the Oxford Record Linkage Study Area. *Health Trends*, volume 22, number 4, pages 166 - 169.

47 R MacFaul and R Long (1991). Major Problems with Paediatric Bed Usage Statistics? *Archives of Disease in Childhood*, volume 66, pages 504 - 507.

48 G N Marsh and D M Channing (1987). Comparison in Use of Health Services Between a Deprived and an Endowed Community. *Archives of Disease in Childhood*, volume 62, pages 392 - 396.

49 British Paediatric Association Working Party (1990). The Organisation of Services for Children with Diabetes. *Diabetic Medicine*, volume 7, pages 457 - 464.

50 D Lessing and M A Tatman (1991). Paediatric Home Care in the 1990s. *Archives of Disease in Childhood*, volume 66, pages 994 - 996

51 Royal College of Nursing of the United Kingdom (1992). *Directory of Paediatric Community Nursing Services*.

52 British Paediatric Association (1992). *Outcome Measures for Child Health*. In press

53 D N Lessing, P G F Swift, M A Metcalfe and J D Baum (1992). Newly Diagnosed Diabetes: a Study of Parental Satisfaction. *Archives of Disease in Childhood*, volume 67, pages 1011 - 1013.

54 Audit Commission for Local Authorities and the National Health Service in England and Wales (1991). *Lying in Wait - The Use of Medical Beds in Acute Hospitals*. HMSO.

55 Audit Commission for Local Authorities and the National Health Service in England and Wales (1992). *Making Time for Patients. A Handbook for Ward Sisters*. HMSO.

56 Sue Dryden (1989). Care in the Community: The Work of Nottingham Paediatric Community Nursing Team. *Paediatric Nursing*, October, pages 19 and 20, November, pages 17 and 18.

57 Welsh Office (1992). *NHS Trusts and Integrated Care*. WHC(92)5

58 British Association of Perinatal Medicine Working Group (1989). Referrals for Neonatal Medical Care in the United Kingdom Over One Year. *British Medical Journal*, 21 January 1989, volume 298, pages 169 - 172.

59 C Amiel-Tison and A Stewart (1989). Follow-up Studies During the First Five Years of Life. A Pervasive Assessment of Neurological Function. *Archives of Disease in Childhood*, volume 64, pages 496 - 502.

Appendices

APPENDIX 1: List of contacts

THE PROJECT ADVISORY GROUP WAS:

John Atwell, Consultant Paediatric & Neonatal Surgeon, Southampton General Hospital.

David Bowden, Managing Director, Merrett Health Risk Management.

Sue Burr, Advisor in Paediatric Nursing, Royal College of Nursing of the United Kingdom.

Professor Richard Cooke, Professor of Child Health, University of Liverpool.

Dr David Field, Senior Lecturer in Child Health, University of Leicester.

Elizabeth Fradd, Senior Nurse Manager Children's Services, University and City Hospitals, Nottingham.

Andrew Freeland, Consultant ENT Surgeon, Radcliffe Infirmary, Oxford.

Professor David Hatch, Portex Professor of Paediatric Anaesthesia, Institute of Child Health, London; Vice President, College of Anaesthetists.

Dr Geoffrey Hatcher, Consultant Paediatrician (retired), Royal Alexandra Hospital for Sick Children, Brighton.

Dr Jacky Hayden, GP, Bury, Greater Manchester.

Professor Sir David Hull, Professor of Child Health, University of Nottingham; President, British Paediatric Association.

Lady Lovell-Davies, Chair, Caring for Children in the Health Services.

Dr Aidan MacFarlane, Consultant Community Paediatrician, Oxfordshire Health Authority.

Dr Roderick MacFaul, Consultant Paediatrician, Pinderfields Hospital, Wakefield; Hon Secretary, British Paediatric Association.

Jerry Read, Child Health, Maternity & Prevention Division, Department of Health.

Anne Rivett, Chairman, Action for Sick Children.

Dr Sheila Shribman, Consultant Community Paediatrician, Northampton Health Authority.

Rosemary Thornes, Project Officer, Caring for Children in the Health Services.

OTHER INDIVIDUALS WHO ASSISTED WITH THE STUDY:
Dr Tony Ducker, Consultant Paediatrician, All Saints Hospital, Chatham, Kent.

Dr Patricia Hamilton, Consultant Paediatrician, St Georges Hospital, London.

Dr Edmund Hey, Consultant Paediatrician, Princess Mary Maternity Hospital, Newcastle Upon Tyne.

ADDITIONAL CONSULTANCY WORK WAS CARRIED OUT BY:
Rosemary Thornes, Project Officer, Caring for Children in the Health Services.

PHOTOGRAPHS WERE SUPPLIED BY:
Action for Sick Children.

Professor Alan Glasper, Professor of Nursing, University of Southampton.

THE MAIN STUDY SITES WERE:
Brighton DHA.

Cornwall DHA.

Gwent DHA.

Liverpool DHA.

North Derbyshire DHA.

Nottingham DHA.

Oxfordshire DHA.

Royal Liverpool Children's Hospital and Community Services NHS Trust.

West Dorset DHA.

West Dorset General Hospitals NHS Trust.

SHORT VISITS WERE ALSO MADE TO:
AMI Portland Hospital for Women and Children, London.

Children's National Medical Center, Washington D. C., USA.

Juliana Children's Hospital, The Hague, Netherlands.

Memorial Hospital, Darlington.

Medway Hospital, Gillingham, Kent.

Northern RHA.

South Western RHA.

The Children's Hospital of Eastern Ontario, Ottawa, Canada.

The Hospital for Sick Children, Toronto, Canada.

The Hospital for Sick Children, Washington D. C., USA.

The Hospitals for Sick Children Special Health Authority.

Wilhelmina Children's Hospital, Utrecht, Netherlands.

THE FOLLOWING ORGANISATIONS WERE CONSULTED ON EARLIER DRAFTS OF THE REPORT:

Action for Sick Children.

Association of British Paediatric Nurses.

Association of Community Health Councils for England and Wales.

British Association of Paediatric Surgeons.

British Association of Perinatal Medicine.

British Medical Association.

British Paediatric Association.

College of Anaesthetists.

College of Health.

College of Ophthalmologists.

Conference of Royal Colleges and their Faculties.

Department of Health.

Institute of Health Services Management.

National Association of Health Authorities and Trusts.

National Children's Bureau.

Neonatal Nurses Association.

NHS Trusts Federation.

Patients Association.

Royal College of General Practitioners.

Royal College of Nursing of the United Kingdom.

Royal College of Physicians.

Royal College of Psychiatrists.

Royal College of Surgeons.

Sick Children's Trust.

Society of Paediatric Anaesthetists.

Society of Public Health.

Trades Union Congress.

Welsh Office.

APPENDIX 2
CO-ORDINATING CHILD HEALTH SERVICES

All children should encounter the child health promotion and disease prevention services when they undergo regular health checks. When they are ill they may see their GP or go to a hospital A&E department. Some children will require secondary and tertiary care as well, and thereby come into contact with many different parts of the NHS and other agencies (Exhibit 23, page 58). Co-ordination of all these services is important so that:

— the role of each part is clear to the children and parents using the services as well as to the staff involved;

— the services are provided in a consistent way with continuity of care;

— wasteful duplication and inefficient use of resources is avoided.

Co-ordination should take place at all levels, within and between hospitals and other agencies, such as local authorities responsible for education and social services. This is what is meant by an integrated child health service (Ref. 3)

Since the Court Report of 1976, much attention has focused on combining parts of the child health services into one management structure as a means of achieving better co-ordination. The BPA have recently defined a 'combined child health service' as including hospital and community secondary care services (Ref. 23).

Combined departments of child health are desirable because they focus attention on the needs of children and options for meeting these needs in whatever setting is most appropriate, without the constraints of reconciling the interests of different providers. But they should not be viewed as either necessary or sufficient for achieving co-ordination in all districts. Appropriate management structures for child health services also depend on local factors like: the volume of the services provided, the size of the providers and their responsibilities for other services, and the geography of the area. The attention given to management structures over recent years has sometimes been at the expense of proper consideration of the underlying objectives and oper-ational co-ordination.

Much can often be done to improve co-ordination within existing management structures. For example: commissioning authorities can contract with a single provider who subcontracts with others, within clear ground rules, and ensures operational co-ordination between them. Also, closer working relationships and joint working groups can be set up between the different providers, greater use can be made of written policies and guidelines to ensure that misunderstand-ings do not occur. These options should be pursued urgently and vigorously, irrespective of any long-term plans to change management structures.

APPENDIX 3
INDICATORS FOR MEASURING QUALITY OF CARE

The audit of services for sick children to be carried out by the Audit Commission's auditors during 1992/93, will include an assessment by them of the quality of care. Auditors will initially check that the policies are written, that they are comprehensive in terms of the principles set out in the chapters on child and family-centred care, specially skilled staff and separate facilities, and that they are being properly implemented and monitored. In addition, a number of specific indicators will be used to check whether the policies are working in practice in wards and A&E departments. These could form the basis, together with other indicators selected by the hospital, of continuous monitoring.

The indicators for wards will be measured from four different perspectives against a specific standard (Exhibit A1, overleaf). The perspectives are:

— objectively measured data;

— the views of children and parents by means of surveys;

— the views of staff by means of interviews;

— observations by the auditor.

These can then be combined into a subjective, but explicit assessment of the quality of care and compared with the standards.

Exhibit A1

TEN INDICATORS FOR MEASURING THE QUALITY OF CARE

Indicator	Standard	Measurement (examples)			
		Objective data	Child/Parent view	Staff view	Auditor Observation
Overall responsibility for ward.	A consultant with overall responsibility	Is there a consultant with overall respnsibility?		Does it work e.g. Is there one consultant who can decide to close the ward in an infection alert?	
Encouragement and support of parents	Encouraged and supported to participate in care.	Does it say so in information leflet?	Do parents feel 'part of the ward team'?	Can parents come and go as they please? Are parents present e.g. - when doctor takes blood.	Are parents staying? - especially parents of under 5s
Nursing Responsibility	One named nurse per patient.	Does it say so in information leaflet?	Do they know they have named nurse?	Do nurses work to this policy? How does handover take place between shifts?	Is there a notice board showing which nurse goes with which child?
Pain relief	Pain preventiion guidelines in place.	Are there written guidelines?	Is child/parent involved in discussions about pain relief?	Do nurses think children have different pain thresholds? How is this assessed?	Are there charts that could be used with young patients to assess pain?
Respect for privacy	Blinds and screens are used in ward.	Do all beds, cubicles and bathrooms have blinds or screens?	Do parents close blinds/screens as they wish?	Do doctors and nurses use blinds/screens before examining a child?	Are there times when children are not given privacy?
Information	Full range of 'high content' leaflets and posters.	Are leaflets readily available, e.g. in out-patient departments for elective admissions?	Has child/parent received a general information leaflet about the ward?	Do staff ask children and parents what information they need?	Are leaflets and notices up to date, relevant and appropriate to the ward and age range?
Junior doctors	Continuous cover by 'experienced' staff.	Assessment of medical rosters.		Ask nurses, how often is the consultant called in? Can junior doctors put up drips and take a lumbar puncture?	Are there regularly times when consultants are the only emergency cover above 'inexperienced' SHO grade?
RSCNs	There should be at least 2 RSCNs on duty per shift.	Assessment of nursing rosters.		Ask senior nurse about RSCN recruitment and retention policy.	How many shifts have no RSCNs or only one on duty?
Ward sensitive to the needs of different ages	Ward imposes no unnecessary rules on children.	Is there a play specialist?	Ask children: : What are the best and worst things about the hospital?	Are children of similar ages put together?	Are a range of basic facilities available for babies, children and adolescents
Facilities for parents	No gaps in facilities.	Are parents able to: make tea or coffee, wash and shower?	Have parents suggested any improvements?	Are there sufficient facilities for all parents who want to stay?	Check facilities.

APPENDIX 4: The decentralisation of tertiary services: neonatal intensive care

Better outcomes for very low birthweight babies (i.e. less than 1500g) and lower costs of providing intensive care, point in the direction of concentrating this care at tertiary centres. But in some regions the growth in intensive care for these babies has been greater at the smaller secondary units (Exhibit 26). There are four main reasons for this:-

(i) **Inaccurate charging for intensive care.**

DHAs using secondary level neonatal units to provide intensive care will often be charged a rate per baby, or per baby-day, averaged across all babies being treated. Such charges are often much lower than equivalent charges for tertiary level units, because the tertiary units provide much more intensive care. Charges at both secondary and tertiary level calculated in this way, bear little resemblance to the true cost of providing intensive care. In fact they suggest that intensive care costs less at secondary level units, when the contrary is true (Ref. 20).

(ii) **Enthusiasm of local paediatricians.**

Intensive care for newborn babies has been one of the growth areas and success stories in paediatrics over recent years (page 39). Many paediatricians want to be part of this success; so much so that some local consultants believe they can provide as good a service for very low birthweight babies as the tertiary centre. The evidence available so far suggests the contrary is true. The onus must therefore be on secondary centres to demonstrate that their outcomes are at least as good as those achieved by the tertiary centres.

(iii) **Parents' desire for care of their baby to be provided locally.**

An important disadvantage of providing neonatal intensive care at tertiary centres is the long distances parents may have to travel to them. It is not surprising, therefore, that parents are often an important source of support for setting up local services.

But parents' desires for local services are often expressed without a clear explanation of the evidence on outcomes. Parents need to be made aware of the trade-off between outcomes and travelling distances. Too often they are given the impression that the quality of intensive care can be just as good locally, with little or no evidence to support this.

(iv) **Lack of space at tertiary centres.**

Some tertiary centres have been unable to accommodate the rapid growth in demand for intensive care (Ref. 58). Some babies have had to be transferred to units outside their home regions and in a few cases it has been impossible to find a place at all. Greater concentration of resources at these centres would assist in overcoming this problem by increasing the number of centres or expanding existing centres. A review of transfer and discharge policies at the tertiary units may also identify a greater scope for the use of secondary care units for babies no longer requiring intensive care. More use could also be made of home care services as a means of achieving earlier discharge.

Exhibit 26
GROWTH IN INTENSIVE CARE DAYS FOR VERY LOW BIRTHWEIGHT BABIES (<1500 G). 1987/88 - 1990/91. NEONATAL UNITS IN 3 REGIONS IN DESCENDING ORDER OF 1987/88 WORKLOAD.
Growth in intensive care days has occurred at most units, but the growth has been greater at units with the lowest workload.

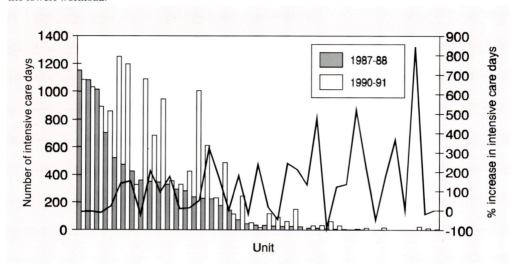

Note: Intensive care is defined here as: continuous supervision by nursing and medical staff, including assisted ventilation.

Source: Trent, Northern and S E Thames regional surveys.

APPENDIX 5: Monitoring outcomes in very low birthweight babies

The prevalence of disabilities amongst very low birthweight babies (i.e less than 1500 grams) who survive, should be monitored by every unit providing this care. This would allow units to assess the effectiveness of their care. If collected in a consistent way at national level, these data could also provide some useful evidence on the long term effects of neonatal intensive care. The Audit Commission has developed a monitoring tool. The tool involves developmental checks at 2 and 4.5 years of age. These checks should be part of the normal checks carried out on children of these ages, but in the case of children who were very low birthweight, should be carried out by a senior paediatrician (SCMO, Consultant or similar) who does not work in the neonatal unit. About 1% of newborn babies are likely to be enroled.

Data should be collected on all babies weighing less than 1,500 grams who are treated in a unit. An individual record for each baby would consist of:

— NHS number (for checking, to avoid double counting) This need not be part of the national database;

— date of birth;

— date of discharge home or death;

— birthweight;

— gestational age;

— gender;

— single, twin or other multiple birth;

— number of days of intensive care (levels 1 and 2 - Ref. 19);

— maternal data:

    mother's date of birth;
    support status;
    age on leaving full time education;

— post-code of mother's residence at time of birth;

— the results of 7 indicators at age 2 years and 4.5 years, adjusted for gestational age (BOX D). These are intended to form a core data set. Additional measures can include:

    illness severity at birth;
    neurological impairment at term;
    other measures of impairment (Ref. 59);
    number of hospital admissions.

Box D
INDICATORS

Cerebral Palsy

(a) Any neuromotor impariment, with disability, due to a brain lesion.
(b) Unable to walk, even with aids.

Developmental delay

Developmental quotient on the Griffiths scale of less than 70 or more than 2 standard deviations below mean for another similar clinical test. This will be corrected for gestational age at 2 years review, but not at 4.5 years review.

Vision

Significant impairment in both eyes. (If measurable, corrected binocular visual acuity of 6/24 or less).

Hearing

Bilateral impairment requiring hearing aid (hearing loss greater than 60dB).

Growth

A weight of more than 2 standard deviations below mean.
A height of more than 2 standard deviations below mean.
A head circumference of more than two standard deviations below mean.

Existence of epilepsy

Needing regular medication.

Other conditions

Any severe continuing condition. Examples: -
    continuously breathless,
    hydrocephalus which has required a shunt,
    stoma,
    loss of a limb.

Glossary

Clinical Medical Officers and Senior Clinical Medical Officers (CMOs and SCMOs)	Doctors who traditionally work outside hospitals complementing the role of GPs in specialised areas of child health surveillance, health promotion and the health care needs of children with disabilities. Their work in primary health surveillance is gradually being taken over by GPs and they are playing a greater role in secondary care services in both hospital and community settings.
Commissioning	Determining the health care needs of a population, specifying the services required to meet these needs, funding providers through a contractual relationship to provide these services and working in co-operation with other agencies (see also *purchasing*).
Extra contractual Referral	Referral to a hospital of a patient from a district or a GP fundholding practice which does not have a contract with that hospital for the services required.
GP fundholders	GPs who have been allocated a budget to purchase certain health care services from hospitals and community units on behalf of their patients.
Hospital and Community Health Services	Services which are the responsibility of District Health Authorities and *GP Fundholders*.
House Officer (HO)	A newly qualified doctor, pre-registration. Does not normally work in paediatrics.
Junior doctors	*House Officers, Senior House Officers, Registrars* and *Senior Registrars*.
Lower Quartile	A point in a frequency distribution which contains 25% of observations below it and 75% of observations above it.
Mortality Rates	The number of deaths in a population over a year compared to the number in that population at some point during that year or the number of births over the same time period.
Named nurse	A specific nurse allocated to oversee the care of a specific child throughout their stay in hospital (*primary nursing*). It can also include allocating nurses for each shift (*team nursing*).
Nebulizer	A powered device for administering inhaled drugs in the treatment of asthma.
Neonatal intensive care	Continuous skilled supervision of newborn babies (up to 28 days old and longer if necessary) by qualified and specially trained nursing and medical staff involving assisted ventilation. Intensive care is some-

	times defined as including procedures other than assisted ventilation (Ref. 19), but they are excluded from this study to clarify the definition.
Neonatal units	Units which provide *intensive care* and *special care* for newborn babies.
Neonatal	The first 28 days of life.
Outcomes	The effects of health care on the health and well being of a child.
Paediatric intensive care	Continuous skilled supervision of babies and children aged over 28 days.
Paediatrics	The branch of medicine dealing specifically with children.
Paediatric Surgery	The branch of surgery dealing specifically with children.
Primary care	Health care and health services provided by GPs or *primary health care teams* working with them.
Primary Health Care Team	GP's, practice nurses, district nurses, health visitors, school nurses and other support staff who work with GPs.
Primary nursing	Nursing philosophy and organisation of care whereby the 'primary nurse' nominated for each child on admission, assumes 24-hour responsibility and authority for all aspects of that child's nursing care during their stay.
Project 2000	Initiative to replace 'apprenticeship' style pre-registration training for nurses with an eighteen month college-based core programme of training, followed by a special 'branch'. The branches include children's nursing.
Purchasing	The process of: (i) specifying health care services to be provided; (ii) negotiating with providers; (iii) paying providers which results from *commissioning;* (iv) monitoring and reviewing performance.
QALYs (Quality Adjusted Life Years)	A measure of the additional life years which may result from health care, adjusted according to a scale of values which takes account of the likely quality of life during those years.
Regional centres	See *tertiary centres.*
Registered General Nurse (RGN)	A nurse qualified in adult general nursing whose name is on parts 1 or 12 of the UK Central Council for Nursing, Midwifery and Health Visiting General Register of Nurses.
Registered Sick Children's Nurse (RSCN)	A nurse qualified in nursing sick children whose name is on parts 8 or 15 of the UK Central Council for Nursing, Midwifery and Health Visiting General Register of Nurses.
Registrar and Senior Registrar	Experienced doctors undertaking higher specialised training.

Rostering	Allocation of shift duties to staff.
Safety net cover	The degree to which junior doctors with at least 12 months experience in paediatrics are resident at a hospital and available to attend an emergency at any time.
Secondary care	Care provided following a referral from the primary care team, a hospital accident and emergency department or a maternity unit.
Senior House Officer (SHO)	A basic grade junior doctor in paediatrics with usually less than 12 months experience in the specialty. A second level junior doctor in other specialties.
Special care baby units	Units which provide *special care for newborn babies*. They must also be able to provide initial care of a baby prior to transfer for neonatal intensive care.
Special care for newborn babies	Care and treatment for newborn babies exceeding normal care (see also, *neonatal intensive care*).
Team nursing	Method of organising nursing care based on allocation of each nurse to a team which cares for a group of patients for a number of shifts.
Tertiary care	Care provided following a referral from a consultant paediatrician, surgeon or GP. It is essentially care that would not normally be provided at a district general hospital because of the relatively small numbers of children involved.
Tertiary centres	Hospital and other centres which provide tertiary care.
Very low birthweight babies	Less than 1500 grams at birth

SOUTH DEVON COLLEGE
LIBRARY